A-LEVEL
STUDENT GUIDE

AQA

Sociology

Education with theory and methods

Dave O'Leary

HODDER
EDUCATION
AN HACHETTE UK COMPANY

**Acknowledgemen~~~~~~~~~~~~~~~~~~~ology students at Kingsthorpe College for their support.

This Guide has been written specifically to support students preparing for the AQA A-level Sociology examinations. The content has been neither approved nor endorsed by AQA and remains the sole responsibility of the author.

Every effort has been made to trace all copyright holders, but if any have been inadvertently overlooked, the Publishers will be pleased to make the necessary arrangements at the first opportunity.

Although every effort has been made to ensure that website addresses are correct at time of going to press, Hodder Education cannot be held responsible for the content of any website mentioned in this book. It is sometimes possible to find a relocated web page by typing in the address of the home page for a website in the URL window of your browser.

Hachette UK's policy is to use papers that are natural, renewable and recyclable products and made from wood grown in well-managed forests and other controlled sources. The logging and manufacturing processes are expected to conform to the environmental regulations of the country of origin.

Orders: please contact Bookpoint Ltd, 130 Park Drive, Milton Park, Abingdon, Oxon OX14 4SE. Telephone: (44) 01235 827827. Fax: (44) 01235 400401. Email: education@bookpoint. co.uk. Lines are open from 9 a.m. to 5 p.m., Monday to Saturday, with a 24-hour message answering service. You can also order through our website: www.hoddereducation.co.uk.

© Dave O'Leary 2020

ISBN 978-1-5104-7202-0

First printed 2020

First published in 2020 by
Hodder Education,
An Hachette UK Company
Carmelite House
50 Victoria Embankment
London EC4Y 0DZ

www.hoddereducation.co.uk

Impression number 10 9 8 7 6 5 4 3 2 1

Year   2024 2023 2022 2021 2020

Cover photo: Dmytro/stock.adobe.com

Typeset by Integra Software Services Pvt. Ltd, Pondicherry, India

Printed in Italy

A catalogue record for this title is available from the British Library.

Contents

Content Guidance

Questions & Answers

■ Getting the most from this book

Exam-style questions

Commentary on the questions

Tips on what you need to do to gain full marks.

Sample student answers

Practise the questions, then look at the student answers that follow.

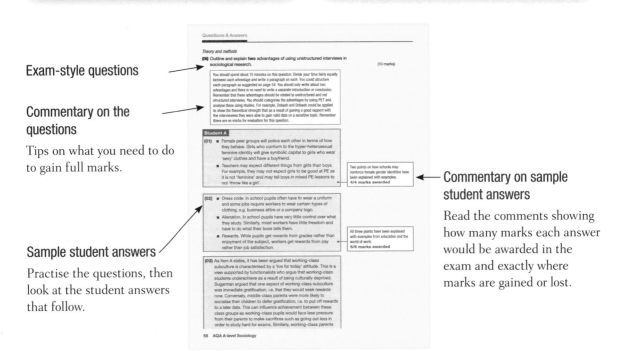

Commentary on sample student answers

Read the comments showing how many marks each answer would be awarded in the exam and exactly where marks are gained or lost.

■About this book

This guide is for students following the A-level Sociology course. It deals with the topics of education and sociological theory and methods. At A-level these are examined in Paper 1, Education with Theory and Methods. The Content Guidance section of this book can also be used by students following the AQA AS Sociology course. This is examined in Paper 1, Education with Methods in Context, and Paper 2 (Section A), Research Methods.

There are two main sections to this guide:

- **Content Guidance** — this provides details for the topics of education and sociological theory and methods. Topic areas on education and theory and methods examine **key ideas** and arguments, stating the main points of evaluation and listing the **key concepts** and **key thinkers**. The defined words are key words for this specification.
- **Questions & Answers** — this shows you the kinds of question you can expect in the A-level Paper 1 examination. There are three test papers followed by sample answers. For the first two papers there are two sets of sample answers, from Student A (A-grade response) and Student B (C-grade response). The third paper has A-grade responses.

How to use this guide

When you study education topics and theory and methods in class, read the corresponding information from the Content Guidance section to become familiar with the topic. You should use this information to complete your own revision notes, for example on each method and topic within education. You will need to complete the question on methods in context after you have finished both the education and the methods topics. It is advisable to focus on one essay question at a time. After you have completed your own answers you should compare them with the answers from Students A and B. These and the commentary can be used to amend your revision notes.

While the test papers have A-level exam questions, question 05 is in the same format as the Methods in Context question in AS Paper 1 and so will also be useful when revising for this exam. Similarly question 04 on the test papers is in the same format as question 05 in AS Paper 1 but is out of 30 rather than 20 marks.

The A-level specification is shown in detail on the AQA website: www.aqa.org.uk/7192. Follow the link to Sociology A-level 7192 (for AS follow 7191).

Content Guidance

◼ The role and functions of education

Functionalism

Key ideas

Functionalists see the role of the education system as positive for both the individual and society. They argue that it has three main functions: socialisation, economic and selection (SES).

Socialisation

- **Durkheim** (1903) argued that education promoted **social solidarity** through creating shared values. Things such as teaching a common history and having assemblies would help bind students together and help create a **value consensus**.
- **Parsons** (1961) argued that education acted as a bridge between the **particularistic** values of the home and the **universalistic** values of society (for example school rules that apply to all students). He felt education was crucial in secondary socialisation and had become the **focal socialising agency**.

Economic

- Durkheim felt that the role of education was to provide not only general values (such as punctuality) but also specific skills (such as numeracy and literacy) needed for the world of work.
- Parsons argued that education socialises young people to believe that society is **meritocratic**. This prepares them for the individualistic and competitive nature of the economy.

Selection

- **Davis and Moore** (1945) argued that the education system helps to 'sift and sort' people into the most appropriate position in the economy (**role allocation**).

> **Exam tip**
>
> Be prepared to link the topic of education to the general theoretical view that functionalists have of society. For example, Parsons argues that education is an important subsystem of the social structure that influences the individual (a 'macro' approach).

Value consensus When there is agreement on key principles and norms in society.

Focal socialising agency The most important mechanism that passes on norms and values.

Meritocratic A meritocracy is when social rewards are based on effort and ability rather than being born into a position. Equal opportunities help ensure status is achieved, not ascribed.

Evaluation

- ■ + Education does perform a key role in secondary socialisation and acts as a bridge between the family and wider society.
- ■ + Education does have an important role in skills provision and allocating future work roles.
- ■ – Marxists have a different view of the three functions:
  - Socialisation. Rather than shared values education transmits ruling-class ideology.
  - Economic. Education reproduces docile, obedient workers for capitalism.
  - Selection. Meritocracy is a myth and the education system legitimates inequality.
- ■ – Interactionists argue that functionalists ignore 'micro' processes in schools.
- ■ – Feminists argue that **patriarchy** within education is ignored. There are not equal opportunities for females in education.

Patriarchy The dominance of men over women.

Knowledge check 1

Outline three ways in which schools can prepare young people for the world of work.

Key concepts

secondary socialisation; social solidarity; value consensus; meritocracy; role allocation

Key thinkers

Durkheim, Parsons, Davis and Moore

Marxism

Key ideas

- ■ **Althusser** argues that education is an **ideological state apparatus** (ISA), a tool used by capitalism to make society seem fair. He argues that education **legitimates** inequality by making it seem that failure is down to the individual rather than being the fault of the school.
- ■ Althusser also argues that the education system **reproduces** class inequality as working-class pupils are likely to end up in the same type of job as their parents.
- ■ **Bowles and Gintis** similarly argue that the **myth of meritocracy** ensures that working-class pupils blame themselves for their failure at school, therefore legitimating class inequality. As a result, they are less likely to try to overthrow capitalism. They argue that there is a **correspondence principle** as school mirrors the world of work — for example, they are both based on hierarchy, rewards, obedience and set routines.
- ■ The **hidden curriculum** (the 'untaught' lessons such as punctuality, accepting the hierarchy of authority and punishments for not doing homework) prepares working-class pupils to accept their role as exploited workers in the capitalist economy. The role of the education system is therefore to reproduce class inequality.

■ **Bourdieu** argues that the education system leads to **cultural reproduction**. Rather than 'sifting and sorting' fairly, schools reward middle-class values. Working-class pupils may lack the **cultural capital** needed for success and so become more likely to end up in working-class jobs. The education system therefore reproduces class inequality.

Evaluation

■ + Statistics and sociological research support the claim that meritocracy is a myth. For example, pupils from working-class backgrounds achieve less well at GCSE.

■ + Demonstrates how individuals within the education system are influenced by structural factors, particularly the economy.

■ + Illustrates how the role of education can be used to pass on ruling-class ideology that supports capitalism.

■ – Internal criticism. Neo-Marxist **Willis** agrees that cultural reproduction occurs but argues that working-class people are active and can see through the myth of meritocracy. The working-class 'lads' developed an anti-school culture which, although it led to their failure, showed how the hidden curriculum can be rejected by pupils.

■ – Functionalists argue that the education system is not controlled by the capitalist economic system but offers equal opportunities for all. It is meritocratic and based on consensus not conflict.

■ – Interactionists argue that (with the exception of Willis) Marxists ignore the role of individuals in education.

■ – Feminists argue that patriarchy within education is ignored. The hidden curriculum reinforces gender inequalities in subject choice, for example.

■ – Postmodernists argue that the Marxist view is out of date and that the correspondence principle does not exist. The role of education in a postmodern society is to ensure diversity not inequality.

Key concepts

ideological state apparatus; legitimation; reproduction; correspondence principle; hidden curriculum; myth of meritocracy; cultural capital

Key thinkers

Althusser, Bowles and Gintis, Bourdieu, Willis

New Right

Key ideas

■ The New Right is a political and sociological perspective that shares and develops some of the ideas of functionalism. See Table 1.

Cultural capital
The middle-class values, knowledge and experiences that are valued by the education system and are required for success in the examination system.

Knowledge check 2

Outline two ways in which cultural capital can lead to middle-class pupils achieving higher levels of attainment than working-class pupils.

Table 1 New Right ideas in relation to functionalism

Similar to functionalist view	Different from functionalist view
Agrees with the selection function. The more talented should be rewarded and allocated the most important jobs.	Education is not fulfilling the economic function. Too few school leavers have the skills needed for the global economy.
Agrees with the socialisation function. Education should pass on shared values to ensure a common culture.	Disagrees that the state can run the education system efficiently to meet the needs of pupils, parents and employers.
Agrees that the education system should be based on meritocracy and competition.	Greater competition is needed to improve standards in the education system.

- Thatcher's government introduced a range of **marketisation** policies in the 1988 **Education Reform Act** (ERA) which were designed to introduce market forces into the education system. **Chubb and Moe** (1990) argued that state-run education needed to be run more like a business with greater competition between schools that had to respond to the needs of their consumers (parents).

- **David** (1993) described marketised education as a 'parentocracy', meaning parents would have the right to choose schools for their children and were given information to do so via **Ofsted reports** and **league tables**.

- Schools were given greater powers to be independent by being able to control their own budgets and to **opt out** of local authority (LA) control. **Open enrolment** meant schools could recruit more pupils and receive greater funding as a result of **formula funding**.

- The New Right advocates greater diversity in the education system and would support the move towards the greater involvement of the private sector (**privatisation**) in the education system such as an increase in the number of academies and business sponsorship.

- In order to respond to the needs of the changing global economy there was also a greater emphasis on **vocational education** in order that young people were more prepared for the world of work (e.g. through vocational A-levels).

Formula funding
Where schools receive funding based on the number of students they attract.

Evaluation

- + Policies influenced by the New Right have made education more responsive to the needs of the economy and created greater diversity in education and training.

- + Supporters argue that the continual improvement in exam results is evidence that increased competition between schools as a result of marketisation policies has improved standards.

- − **Ball** argues that there is a 'myth of parentocracy' and that in reality middle-class parents benefit from marketisation policies. As **Gerwitz** suggests, working-class parents may lack the cultural and economic capital to be 'skilled choosers'.

- − Marketisation has created an unequal, 'two-tier' state education system. Whereas popular schools are better funded and can attract more able, usually middle-class pupils, 'failing schools' cannot afford to be selective and may find it difficult to improve performance due to reduced funding and their inability to attract more able pupils.

Key concepts

marketisation; parentocracy; consumer choice; competition; privatisation; formula funding

Knowledge check 3

Outline three criticisms of the marketisation of education.

Postmodernism

Key ideas

- The economy has moved from being **Fordist** (based on assembly-line mass production) to **post-Fordist** (which is increasingly **fragmented** and has to respond to the needs of the global market).
- The role of the education system has similarly had to shift from a 'one size fits all' provision (typified by comprehensive schools popular in the 1960s, see page 24) to the **diverse** range of education and training that reflects consumer choice and the needs of the ever-changing economy.
- Postmodernists point to the impact that **globalisation** has had on society, the economy and the education system. For example, many academy chains (see page 26) are controlled by companies from the USA, which has resulted in American-based behaviour management policies and teaching techniques being implemented. The increase in the number of overseas students has had an impact on the types of courses offered in higher education (e.g. more in medical sciences).
- Postmodernists argue that 'modern' theories such as functionalism and Marxism are out of date because of factors such as globalisation. They are particularly critical of Marxists such as Bowles and Gintis as they see the economy and the education system as diverse rather than based on class inequality.

Globalisation
The increased interconnectedness in the world, characterised by international corporations and the global media.

Exam tip

Be prepared to link factors such as the increase in globalisation and privatisation and relate them to sociological theory. For example, New Right policies that have led to the increased influence of the private sector have brought about the diversity in the education system suggested by postmodernists, such as the growth of academies.

Evaluation

- + Postmodernists are right to point out that society has become more diverse and that the economy requires workers to be more adaptable and have transferable skills.
- + Recent government and school policies have reflected increased diversity and flexibility in educational provision (e.g. specialist schools, academies, free schools, faith schools, lifelong learning, personalised timetables).
- – Marxists argue that postmodernists ignore class inequality in the education system and wider society.
- – Education is still largely under state control; is it really that diverse?

Knowledge check 4

Outline two criticisms of the postmodern view that the education system is characterised by diversity.

Key concepts

diversity; fragmentation; globalisation; post-Fordism

Summary

After studying this section, you should be able to explain the role and purpose of education, including its relationship to the economy and to the class structure. You should be familiar with the main perspectives:

- Functionalism focuses on the positive contributions of the education system in maintaining social order in society and preparing and allocating individuals to their future role in the economy.
- Marxism focuses on how the education system oppresses pupils and reproduces and legitimates inequality between the social classes.

- The New Right emphasises how the marketisation of the education system is required in order that it meets the needs of pupils, parents and the economy.
- Postmodernists argue that the education system has developed to reflect the diverse needs of a post-Fordist economy.
- Feminists argue that all other theories ignore gender inequalities and that the education system reproduces patriarchal power in society.

■ Class differences in achievement

Social class has a significant impact on a child's educational achievement. Students from professional backgrounds are significantly more likely to achieve five A*–C grades (or Grade 4 and above) at GCSE and enter higher education than those from unskilled backgrounds. As well as being more likely to stay in education longer, middle-class pupils are more likely to start school being able to read than pupils from disadvantaged backgrounds. Different reasons have been put forward for this social class gap in achievement.

External factors

Material deprivation

- This involves a lack of money to afford basic necessities.
- Working-class families are much more likely to be in poverty due to factors such as unemployment or a low income. They therefore may lack the money to afford resources which help academic success, such as internet access, school trips and study books. Bull (1980) refers to this as 'the cost of free schooling'.
- They will be less able to afford private tuition and higher education costs.
- As Howard (2001) notes, poor diet can lead to absence through ill health and to low levels of concentration.
- Poor living conditions can lead to poor health and absence from school. They can also mean a lack of space to study due to overcrowding.
- Government statistics show that those receiving free school meals consistently underachieve, demonstrating the correlation between material deprivation and lower rates of academic success.

Cultural deprivation

- Cultural deprivation refers to a lack of the 'correct' values, attitudes and skills needed for academic success. Cultural deprivation theorists argue that working-class parents often fail to socialise their children into these values.

> **Exam tip**
>
> Be prepared to evaluate each of these factors by referring to various policies and interventions aimed at tackling material deprivation, such as bursaries, student grants for higher education, schools subsidising school trips, and schools and public libraries lending textbooks.

> **Knowledge check 5**
>
> Outline three material factors that may negatively affect the educational achievement of working-class students.

- Sociologists such as functionalists and the New Right would argue that working-class culture (and underclass culture for the New Right) and parenting are not sufficiently aimed at educational success.
- Cultural deprivation theorists would maintain that, compared to their middle-class counterparts, working-class parents are less likely to encourage **intellectual development** by reading to their children or engaging in educational activities.
- **Douglas** (1964) argued that working-class parents had lower aspirations. He claimed that this was demonstrated by the fact that they were less likely than middle-class parents to go to parents' evenings.
- **Sugarman** (1970) argued that working-class culture was characterised by values such as **immediate gratification** (wanting rewards now) and **fatalism** that acted as a barrier to achievement. For example, working-class parents would be more likely to encourage their children to leave school as soon as possible in order to earn money.
- Conversely, middle-class parents would encourage their children to **defer gratification** (postpone rewards) by staying in education as long as possible to gain qualifications.
- **Bernstein** (1970) argued that working-class people may underachieve as they tend to use only the **restricted code** which is based on short forms of speech, whereas the middle class tend to be socialised into the **elaborated code** which is the language used by teachers and the school curriculum. Therefore, middle-class students are more likely to achieve, particularly in subjects such as English.

Fatalism The idea that there is nothing you can do to change your situation (such as working hard in school).

Theories of cultural and material deprivation have had an influence on government policy in the form of **compensatory education** in the 1960s. Operation Head Start in the USA was influenced by cultural deprivation theory and was aimed at changing the values of low-income parents in order to better prepare preschool children for school. In the UK compensatory education began with **Educational Priority Areas** where the government allocated additional resources to four low-income inner-city areas. More recently New Labour attempted to tackle **social exclusion** with policies such as **Education Action Zones** and **Sure Start** (see page 25).

Social exclusion
Social exclusion is where individuals or groups of people are blocked from rights, opportunities and resources that are normal for other members of society. Policies to combat social exclusion aim to reintegrate excluded people back into society.

Exam tip

You should make the link between sociological theory and government educational policies. Compensatory policies such as Operation Head Start were based on the functionalist belief that educational underachievement was caused by poor socialisation at home.

Cultural capital

- Marxist **Bourdieu** (1971, 1984) argued that middle-class pupils achieve more as they possess the language, values and skills that are rewarded by the education system. This he called **cultural capital**. For example, a knowledge of Shakespeare and 'the arts', which upper- and middle-class parents may have socialised their children into, will be rewarded and seen as valuable by schools.
- Bourdieu argued that, as well as having more economic capital (i.e. financial resources), middle-class people are more likely to possess the cultural capital needed to succeed in education. He also argued that this was passed on from one generation to the next, resulting in **cultural reproduction**.

Knowledge check 6

What is the difference between cultural capital and cultural deprivation?

Evaluation

Table 2 A comparison of cultural and material explanations

Cultural deprivation	Material deprivation
Douglas suggests that middle-class parents may have higher aspirations for their children due to their own higher levels of education. If a child's parent does not attend a parents' evening, this may send the message that the child does not need to try hard at school.	Is attending parents' evenings a good measure of parental interest? Working-class parents may not attend due to having to work shifts or may not be able to afford the costs of attending such as transport or babysitting. They may also be put off by what they feel is the middle-class atmosphere of the school.
Sugarman argues that middle-class parents are likely to socialise their children to defer gratification and will place a higher value on education as they themselves are more likely to have gone to university.	Working-class people are being realistic, not fatalistic. Rather than not valuing education, they may have no choice but to ask their children to leave school as they need them to earn money for the family.
Cultural deprivation theorists would argue that a poor diet is based more on cultural choices than a lack of money.	Working-class families may not be able to afford the healthy diet that is essential to help children achieve.
Cultural deprivation theorists argue that would parents not buying educational toys may have a negative impact on developing children's intellectual skills and hence achievement.	Working-class parents may not buy educational toys because they are more expensive, not because they are not interested in developing their children intellectually.

- ■ + A strength of **Bernstein** is that, unlike other cultural deprivation theorists, he acknowledges that the school has a role in working-class underachievement. He argues that the school is to blame for not teaching them the elaborated code. However, the significance of possessing the elaborated code may not be as great in some subjects, such as maths.
- ■ – **Keddie** (1973) criticises cultural deprivation for adopting a 'victim-blaming' approach. She argues that working-class culture is different, not inferior. The same criticism can be applied to ideas about working-class language codes.
- ■ + A strength of **Bourdieu** is that he emphasised the importance of both cultural and economic factors. However, material deprivation theorists argue that he overestimates the importance of cultural factors. For example, rather than a lack of cultural capital, a lack of money is more likely to prevent a working-class student from going to university due to maintenance costs and the potential need to repay expensive tuition fees. Also, is culture automatically passed on, as Bourdieu suggests?
- ■ – Not all working-class students fail and external explanations ignore the impact of school-based factors.

Internal factors

Interactionists look at a range of processes within school that can affect differential class achievement.

Labelling

Becker (1971) argued that teachers (who are mainly middle class) evaluated pupils in terms of an '**ideal pupil**', reflecting middle-class attitudes, values and speech codes. Working-class pupils were more likely to be negatively labelled by teachers and seen as '**deviant pupils**'.

Self-fulfilling prophecy

Rosenthal and Jacobsen (1968) argued that negative labelling can lead to a **self-fulfilling prophecy** of failure. If students are negatively labelled by a teacher they may develop a negative self-image, see themselves as failures, and so give up and underachieve.

> **Exam tip**
>
> These factors can also be applied to differential achievement based on ethnicity and gender.

> **Self-fulfilling prophecy** When people act out a label: they behave in the way they know others have predicted.

Streaming

Due to labelling, working-class pupils are more likely to be put in a lower **stream** and so to underachieve. **Keddie** (1971) felt that, by being placed in lower streams, working-class pupils were being denied the knowledge they needed for success.

Gillborn and Youdell (2001) argued that the pressure on schools to improve their league table position (the **A-to-C economy**) led to the adoption of a different form of streaming. Educational triage occurred where no help was given to students viewed as 'hopeless cases', whereas additional resources such as mentoring support were given to pupils on the C/D border. As a result of labelling, working-class (and black) students were more likely to be placed in bottom sets and sit lower-tier GCSEs, even though they had similar grades to middle-class and white students.

Subculture

- **Lacey** (1970) argued that, as a response to labelling, **polarisation** occurs whereby those positively labelled by teachers (mainly middle-class pupils) adopt a **pro-school** subculture, whereas those negatively labelled (mainly working-class pupils) adopt an **anti-school** subculture which leads to failure.
- **Woods** (1984) adopted a more sophisticated approach and argued that there were eight types of **pupils' adaptations** to labelling and streaming. For example, 'compliance' was mainly a pro-education response but pupils would only comply with teachers for their own reasons, such as exam success.

Marxist views of processes within school:

- A study by **Willis** showed how the anti-school culture of the working-class 'lads' meant that they would fail and end up in working-class jobs. This subculture did not result from teacher labelling, however, but from these pupils' manual working-class values.
- **Bowles and Gintis** argued that the correspondence principle and the hidden curriculum, with their emphasis on competition and accepting authority, were processes in school that favoured middle-class students and prepared them for their future roles, such as managerial positions (see page 7).

Identity: class and achievement

- Identity refers to how individuals see themselves and how they are seen by others. It is complex and shaped not only by factors such as gender, class and ethnicity but also by issues such as sexuality and different types of consumption and leisure patterns. **Hollingsworth and Williams** (2009) found that male working-class subcultures are now seen by other pupils (not themselves) as 'chavs' rather than 'lads' and that mainly middle-class subcultures such as 'emos', 'goths' and 'skaters' are influenced by different genres of music. As Willis's study on the 'lads' demonstrates, working-class identities can have a negative impact on achievement.
- **Archer et al.** (2010) argued that the identity of working-class pupils is based on ways of thinking that can be very different from the middle-class **habitus** of the school. While dress styles such as 'low-riding' trousers, baseball caps and sports designer wear (e.g. Nike) may generate self-worth for the working-class pupil, this

Streaming When schools group students together by ability for all subjects.

Polarisation Where two opposite extremes are created. For example, teacher labelling may lead to students joining two types of subculture, pro- or anti-school.

Exam tip

Be prepared to make links between sociological theory and methods (see page 27). Willis is described as a neo-Marxist as he combines Marxist theory with interpretivist methods favoured by interactionists. By using group interviews and observation, Willis felt he was able to uncover the meanings behind why the 'lads' resisted the values of school.

Habitus A term developed by Bourdieu to describe socialised norms or tendencies that guide behaviour and thinking and are shared by a particular social class.

would conflict with the dress codes of the school. Conversely, middle-class pupils are likely to have been socialised into cultural experiences valued by the school. Bourdieu (1984) argued that as a result they are likely to gain **symbolic capital** (or status) from teachers.

■ Archer et al. (2010) argued that many working-class pupils see education as being alien to them and feel that in order to be successful they would have to 'give up' their working-class identity, which they recognise as being devalued by the school. As a result, some may choose **self-exclusion** from typical middle-class lifestyle choices such as higher education but instead actively 'resist through rituals' by heavily investing in their **'Nike identity'**. This conflict with the school's habitus has a negative impact on the achievement of working-class students who choose not to conform to it. As Bourdieu suggests, working-class pupils may not see high-status universities as being 'for the likes of us' so will not be motivated to achieve.

Policies

In addition to the above internal factors, **educational policies** also influence processes in schools and affect differential class achievement. Sociologists such as Marxists would argue that marketisation policies, with their emphasis on greater selection, have increased the class gap in achievement (see page 24). **Bartlett** (1993) argues that these policies enable schools high up in the league tables to 'cream-skim' higher-ability students who are more likely to be middle class. They can also 'silt-shift' less able students to schools lower in the league tables. These less able students are more likely to be working-class pupils who will then have less opportunity to be successful in a lower-achieving school.

Evaluation of internal explanations

■ + Interactionists demonstrate the importance of how labelling and other processes in schools can lead to inequalities in achievement between the social classes. They highlight a range of different strategies that students can adopt, which enable them to achieve status through alternative means.

■ – Internal criticism. Labelling and the self-fulfilling prophecy are too **deterministic**. As **Fuller**'s study shows, students can reject negative teacher labels and achieve (see page 19). Rather than a self-fulfilling prophecy of failure, students can adopt a self-negating prophecy of success.

■ – Cultural deprivation theorists argue that subcultures develop from the values of working-class people rather than processes in schools.

■ – Marxists argue that interactionists fail to take account of external factors, namely how differential class achievement is caused by inequalities in capitalist society.

■ – Interactionist research is not representative as it is usually based on the experiences of one school so cannot be generalised.

Knowledge check 7

Outline two criticisms of the view that teacher labelling results in pupils joining anti-school subcultures.

Exam tip

Be prepared to evaluate evidence by showing its relevance to contemporary issues in education. While streaming is less common now than in the 1970s, when interactionist research was prominent, working-class pupils today may still be more likely to be placed in lower sets and therefore entered for lower-tier exams.

Deterministic Taking the view that human behaviour is directed and determined by forces beyond the control of the individual.

Summary

After studying this section, you should be able to explain differential educational achievement of social groups by social class in contemporary society and the relationships and processes within schools in relation to social class. You should be familiar with the following suggested explanations:

- external factors including material deprivation, cultural deprivation, language codes and cultural capital
- internal factors including processes in schools such as teacher–pupil relationships, labelling, pupil identities and subcultures, and the organisation of teaching and learning, setting and streaming, the curriculum (both official and hidden) and educational policies

Ethnic differences in achievement

In terms of ethnic groups, the highest achievers historically have been students from Chinese, African Asian (Indian in origin) and Indian backgrounds. Students from black, Pakistani and Bangladeshi backgrounds have performed less well, although more recently Bangladeshi students have achieved higher levels than white British students. However, differential ethnic achievement is a very complex issue and is also influenced by social class and gender. For example, both black and white working-class boys are statistically more likely to be low achievers while Bangladeshi and Pakistani women are the least well qualified.

External factors

Material deprivation

Material deprivation theorists argue that there is a link between a lack of financial resources and achievement.

- As Pakistani and Bangladeshi pupils are from the poorest ethnic groups, they are more likely to be affected by a lack of material resources.
- The **Swann Report** (1985) judged that socioeconomic factors affected the lower levels of achievement of black-Caribbean pupils.
- As Chinese, African Asian and Indian pupils are less likely to be from a family affected by low income or unemployment, they are less likely to experience material deprivation.
- The discrimination that is often experienced by minority ethnic groups (MEGs) in the wider society, in employment and housing in particular, may contribute to the levels of material deprivation experienced. For example, Woods et al. (2010) found that almost half as many 'ethnic minority' as 'white' fictitious applicants were offered a job interview by employers (they sent written job application forms from fictitious applicants).

Exam tip

For an essay question on class and achievement, be prepared to discuss how internal and external factors may be interrelated. For example, teacher labels (an internal factor) may be based on external factors such as language codes used by pupils. Pupil identities can also be shaped by external factors such as the 'Nike identity' and internal factors such as verbal abuse from peers.

Exam tip

Many of the external factors that affect class and achievement (see page 11) can be applied to MEGs. For example, some cultural deprivation theorists would argue that low-income black families do not intellectually stimulate their children and instead socialise them into values such as immediate gratification and fatalism. The same evaluation points on these factors can therefore also be applied to ethnicity (see page 13).

Cultural deprivation

Cultural deprivation theorists have argued that there is a link between a lack of the 'correct' values and low levels of educational achievement.

- Lupton (2004) argued that white working-class pupils are among the lowest-achieving groups due to a lack of parental support and negative attitudes towards education (see also page 12).
- Cultural deprivation theorists argue that children from black and other MEG backgrounds often have a lack of Standard English and so are at a disadvantage in school. Bereiter and Engelmann (1966) judged that the language of low-income black Americans was a barrier to achievement in school.
- **Murray** (1984) argued that many black boys underachieved due to not having a male role model at home as a higher proportion of black-Caribbean families were single-parent families at that time.
- **Pryce** (1979) described the structure of black-Caribbean families as 'turbulent' and argued that, compared with Asian culture, black-Caribbean culture was less resistant to racism, which meant that black pupils might lack self-esteem and so underachieve.

Knowledge check 8

Outline three cultural factors that may affect the achievement of at least two different MEGs.

Evaluation of external factors

- + The **Swann Report** found that at least half of the difference in achievement between ethnic groups was due to social class, supporting the importance of material deprivation.
- + Language barriers are likely to affect the achievement of pupils whose first language is not English, particularly those who have recently migrated to the UK.
- – Material deprivation does not explain all differences between ethnic groups. For example, white and Asian middle-class pupils do better than black middle-class pupils.
- – Research suggests that language is not a key factor. **Driver and Ballard** (1981) found that Asian pupils whose first language was not English had caught up by the age of 16. Also, schools offer additional support for students whose first language is not English (referred to as EAL support — English as an additional language).
- – **Connor** (2004) found that parents from all MEGs placed a higher value on the importance of their children attending higher education than white parents.
- – Female-headed households with independent, career-minded black-Caribbean women may act as a positive role model for black girls, helping them to achieve.
- – **Khan** (1979) argued that Asian families are 'controlling', particularly for girls, and that this may act as a barrier to success rather than being a positive resource.
- – Not all parents from MEG backgrounds could be said to suffer from cultural deprivation. 'Tiger mums', with their emphasis on the importance of education, may help to explain the high achievement of Chinese pupils. **Driver and Ballard** (1981) judged that Asian families were a 'positive resource' due to high levels of parental expectations which increased achievement levels.

- – **Mirza** (1992) found that it was not a lack of self-esteem that caused black girls to underachieve. The group she studied had a pro-education subculture, but they failed as they were unwilling to ask for help from teachers, whom they saw as racist.
- – **Keddie** is critical of cultural deprivation theory (see page 14) and argues that MEGs cannot be deprived of their own culture. She argues that internal factors, such as schools being ethnocentric, are the cause of MEGs underachieving.
- – The average GCSE Attainment 8 score in 2017 for Chinese girls who receive free school meals (60.9) was higher than that for white girls who did not receive them (50.4). This suggests that cultural factors may be more important than material factors.

Exam tip

Be prepared to link external to internal factors. While disagreeing with cultural deprivation theorists, interactionists argue that teachers may negatively label students who have English as a second language or who have a different accent as having less ability and therefore place them in lower sets.

Internal factors

Labelling

- **Gillborn and Youdell** (2000) found that teachers had 'racialised expectations' which resulted in black students being negatively labelled as a 'threat'. They felt that black boys were more likely to be excluded or put in bottom sets as a result.
- **Wright** (1992) found that Asian pupils were excluded and received less attention from teachers, having been labelled as having poor language skills. They failed as a result of the negative impact this had on their self-esteem.

Exam tip

As with social class, you should be prepared to analyse how concepts such as labelling, self-fulfilling prophecy, subcultures and streaming interact and relate to ethnicity and achievement. If MEG students are negatively labelled they may be more likely to be placed in a lower set or stream, join an anti-school subculture and underachieve as a result.

Pupil identities

- From interviews and focus groups with teachers, pupils and parents in secondary schools, **Archer** (2008) found that MEGs were excluded from the ideal pupil identity, which was seen as white, middle-class, male and 'normal' in terms of sexuality. Despite being successful, Chinese pupils were viewed as being too passive, quiet and repressed (females) or effeminate (males) and therefore the 'wrong' sort of learner.
- Archer identified two other pupil identities: the 'pathologised' (abnormal), which was the hard-working, conformist Asian pupil with an oppressed sexuality; and the 'demonised', which was the culturally and intellectually inferior black or white working-class pupil with an inappropriate, 'excessive' sexuality. Archer's study illustrated the complex nature of the beliefs held by teachers regarding pupil identities, which involved an interplay between ethnicity, class, gender and sexuality. These beliefs about different ethnic identities may impact on the achievement of different MEGs.

Subcultures

- **Sewell** (1988) found that there were four types of pupil responses that black boys would adapt to as a result of being negatively labelled by teachers as anti-school. The 'rebels' lived up to this label, formed an anti-school subculture and failed. However, this response was rare and the largest group was the 'conformists' who adopted pro-school attitudes and worked hard to achieve.
- Like Sewell's 'innovators', **Fuller's** (1984) black girls adopted a pro-education, anti-school subculture and worked hard to achieve but rejected teacher labels and didn't seek their approval.

Institutional racism

Troyna and Williams (1986) argued that, as well as individual racism in schools, the achievement of different ethnic groups is influenced by **institutional racism**. Critical race theorists such as **Roithmayr** (2003) have argued that institutional racism is a 'locked-in inequality'. Institutional racism in schools may take several forms, affecting the curriculum, educational policies or assessment.

Institutional racism
Where the policies and attitudes of an institution, such as a school or college, unintentionally discriminate against MEGs.

The ethnocentric curriculum

- Some sociologists have argued that the curriculum in British schools reflects white, middle-class culture over others. Subjects such as history and religious education are seen as being taught from a British, Christian perspective and have marginalised the history of ethnic minorities.
- **Coard** (1971) argued that the ethnocentric curriculum is an example of institutional racism in British schools which makes black students feel inferior and lowers their self-esteem and achievement as a result.

Educational policies

Gillborn (1997) argued that marketisation policies allowing increased selection can be viewed as another form of institutional racism as they may discriminate against certain MEGs. For example, black-Caribbean pupils, particularly boys, may be seen as 'less attractive' to higher-achieving schools due to their perceived negative impact on a school's league table position. As a result, their achievement may be negatively affected as a result of going to less popular, 'failing' schools.

> **Exam tip**
>
> As Evans (2006) argues, when looking at ethnicity and achievement you should be prepared to discuss the interplay between ethnicity, class and gender. While class may be less significant for the lower achievement of black boys, it may have an impact on the achievement of Indian girls.

Assessment and the 'new IQism'

Gillborn (2008) argued that methods used to assess students' ability can be institutionally racist as they may be based on teachers' racist assumptions, such as black pupils being a 'threat'. As a result, pupils from black African or Caribbean backgrounds have been less likely to be given access to equal opportunity measures, such as the 'Gifted and Talented' programme, and have been more likely to be placed in lower sets and entered for lower exam tiers.

Evaluation of internal factors

- – As with social class (see page 15), a problem with teacher labelling as an explanation for ethnic differences in underachievement is that it is deterministic as the self-fulfilling prophecy may not occur. As the studies by **Mirza**, **Fuller** and **Sewell** illustrate, students may respond to teacher labels in a variety of different ways.
- – Cultural deprivation theorists would argue that higher exclusion rates for black boys are caused by more instances of poor behaviour, stemming from inadequate socialisation, rather than by teacher labelling or institutional racism.
- – Other external factors may also be an important cause of underachievement. **Sewell** argues that, while teacher labelling may influence the achievement of some black boys (particularly the 'rebels'), a more important factor is the absence of positive role models and a lack of 'tough love'. He argues that, as well as a lack of a male role model at home, some black boys may be influenced by the macho, 'gangsta' image of black males which is promoted by the media and which does not place value on educational success.
- – Internal explanations also ignore the impact that racism in wider society may have on achievement.
- – Some reject the claim that the British education system is institutionally racist and that the curriculum is ethnocentric. For example, multicultural education policies have been introduced into schools and multicultural content is included in subjects such as religious education, which teaches about world religions as part of the National Curriculum. Also, Chinese students are the highest-achieving ethnic group despite their culture being largely ignored in the curriculum.

Exam tip

You can develop evaluation by referring to different theoretical criticisms of factors that affect achievement. In terms of selection policies, Marxist-influenced sociologists would argue that, rather than being culturally deprived through factors such as language barriers, MEGs may lack the cultural capital required to get their children into the higher-achieving schools.

Knowledge check 9

Outline two examples of institutional racism that may affect the achievement of MEGs.

Summary

After studying this section, you should be able to explain the differential educational achievement of social groups by ethnicity in contemporary society and the relationships and processes within schools relating to ethnicity. You should be familiar with the following:

- external factors including material deprivation, cultural deprivation, language codes, cultural capital and racism in wider society
- internal factors including processes in schools such as teacher–pupil relationships, labelling, pupil identities and subcultures, the organisation of teaching and learning, setting and streaming, the ethnocentric curriculum and educational policies

Gender differences in achievement and subject choice

While boys previously achieved higher than girls, since the 1980s they have fallen behind. Girls are now achieving better results than boys at every level and in most subjects. Despite this, there are still some gender differences in subject choice, particularly at post-16. While boys tend to choose subjects such as science and technology, for example, girls tend to opt for arts-and-humanities-based subjects.

Tables 3a and 3b show external and internal factors that help to explain the 'gender gap' in achievement. The factors (AO1) are listed in the left-hand columns, while the right-hand columns show possible ways in which each factor could be developed with AO2 (application to achievement) or AO3 points. (See page 46 for more specific information on assessment objectives.)

Exam tip

For questions on boys' underachievement, you should refer to the fact that, while the gender gap has increased over the past 40 years, boys' achievement has also increased considerably over this period.

The 'gender gap' in achievement

Table 3a External factors that help to explain the 'gender gap' in achievement

External factors	Assessment objectives (AOs)
The influence of feminism This has raised awareness about gender inequality in society. 'Girl power' has made girls more independent.	**AO2** This has caused a change in female expectations which has made girls value education more. **AO3** Radical feminists argue that patriarchy still exists.
Changing priorities Sharpe (1994) found that between 1974 and 1994 girls' priorities switched from love and marriage to careers and supporting themselves.	**AO2** This change in aspirations, with the desire to be financially independent, requires girls to work hard in school in order to gain qualifications.
Changes in the family The number of female lone-parent families has increased.	**AO2** 'Working mums' act as role models and do inspire girls to achieve.
Changes in women's employment Legislation such as the Equal Pay and Sex Discrimination Acts has created more equality and increased the proportion of women in employment.	**AO2** Increased opportunities in employment have given the incentive for girls to work hard in school. **AO3** The pay gap between the sexes still exists. There is still a glass ceiling in many employment sectors.

Table 3b Internal factors that help to explain the 'gender gap' in achievement

Internal factors	Assessment objectives (AOs)
Educational policies Governments have introduced a range of policies that have led to equal opportunities for girls in education.	**AO2/3** GIST (Girls into Science and Technology) and the National Curriculum (see page 24) have improved girls' participation and achievement in subjects such as science. Barriers have been removed.
Positive role models in schools The number of female teachers and head teachers has increased.	**AO3** While the majority of heads at primary level are female, most secondary heads are male.
Changes in assessment AS and A-levels and GCSEs introduced more coursework and modular exams which favoured girls.	**AO2** Coursework did raise girls' achievement due to girls typically being more organised than boys. **AO3** More recent changes have meant less coursework and a return to final exams.
Teacher labelling Research suggests that teachers have lower expectations of boys and give more positive attention to girls.	**AO2** This may lead to a self-fulfilling prophecy of failure for boys but raise the achievement of girls. **AO3** This research is dated and may not apply today.
Fewer stereotypes in the curriculum Gender stereotypes were removed from resources.	**AO2** Fewer sexist images of females in textbooks may raise aspirations and therefore achievement of girls.
Selection policies Marketisation policies (see page 24) have meant that boys are less attractive to higher-achieving schools.	**AO2** Girls are more likely to get into a 'good' school and so have a greater opportunity to achieve than boys.

Table 4 shows external and internal factors that relate to boys' underachievement.

Table 4 Factors that relate to the underachievement of boys

External factors	Assessment objectives (AOs)
Boys' lack of literacy skills While girls tend to have a 'bedroom culture' which promotes literacy and communication skills, boys typically read less and tend to engage in more active leisure activities.	**AO2** If reading is seen by boys as 'girly' it will have a negative impact in some subjects, especially English. **AO3** There have been policies introduced to encourage boys to read, e.g. 'Reading Champions'.
Fewer 'male' jobs As a result of globalisation there has been a decline in the number of traditional 'male' jobs in manufacturing. Boys are having an 'identity crisis' as they may no longer be future breadwinners.	**AO2** The rise in male unemployment may lead to boys not seeing the point of education and failing. **AO3** Will boys make the connection between working hard in school and the types of jobs they wish to do when they leave school?
Lack of male role models at home Due to changes in the family.	**AO3** Does this mean that boys value education less?
Internal factors	Assessment objectives (AOs)
Feminisation of education This is seen in the use of coursework and in a lack of male teachers, particularly at primary level.	**AO3** Francis (2006) found that the gender of teachers was not important to most primary school students.
Laddish subcultures Mac an Ghaill (1994) argues that boys are more likely than girls to join anti-school subcultures. As with Willis's 'lads', these subcultures may be caused by external factors.	**AO2** If boys are more concerned about being negatively labelled by peers (e.g. as 'gay') if they try hard in school, this will reduce achievement. **AO3** This may apply more to working-class boys.

Subject choice

Table 5 shows external and internal factors affecting gender and subject choice.

Table 5 Factors affecting gender and subject choice

External	AO2: Application to subject choice
Early gender socialisation Norman (1988) notes how sex stereotyping occurs in terms of the types of toys bought and the types of play that boys and girls are encouraged to engage in.	If boys are given construction-based toys they are more likely to opt for resistant materials at GCSE. Conversely, if girls are given dolls and kitchen sets they are more likely to pick health and social care.
Gendered career opportunities Sex stereotyping occurs in jobs, such as IT being seen as a male domain and the 'caring' professions being seen as for females.	As a result, boys and girls are more likely to opt for subjects that relate to these careers, such as childcare and food technology for girls and computing for boys.
Gendered subject images Kelly (1987) felt that science was presented as a masculine subject by teachers. Research suggests that subjects such as science are taught in ways that favour boys.	As a result, girls are less likely to opt for science subjects. However, in single-sex schools, more girls opt for traditional 'male' subjects, which suggests the school may have an influence on subject images.
Peer pressure Pupils are likely to be influenced by their peers to choose gender-stereotypical subjects. Dewar (1990) found that girls were called 'butch' if they picked PE as an option.	Boys may be less likely to opt for subjects such as dance if they are called 'gay' by their friends. However, such stereotypes are increasingly less common today.

Exam tip

In an essay question on achievement in relation to either gender, class or ethnicity, be prepared to state which factor you feel is the most important influence. This would be a useful strategy to employ in a conclusion.

Exam tip

You can also develop analysis by explaining how factors that influence subject choice may link together. For example, as the image of subjects such as dance becomes less stereotypically female, it is less likely that boys will receive negative comments from their peers if they opt for them.

Gender identities

- **Radical feminists** argue that schools reinforce gender and sexual identities, which helps to promote a **hegemonic masculinity**. **Lees** (1986 and 1993) identified how this occurs through **double standards** and **verbal abuse**. Whereas girls were negatively labelled as 'slags', 'sluts' and 'slappers', boys would be viewed as 'studs' for the same sexual behaviour. Lees argued that these double standards and name-calling helped to shape and justify male power. Research suggests that verbal abuse of girls was often ignored and unchallenged by teachers, therefore reinforcing hegemonic definitions of gender identity.

- Verbal abuse may also be used to reinforce masculine identities by male peer groups. **Mac an Ghaill** (1994) found that working-class 'macho lads' referred to working-class boys who worked hard as 'dickhead achievers'. **Epstein** (1998) and **Willis** showed how working-class boys who want to achieve may be the victims of verbal abuse and be labelled as effeminate or 'gay'.

- In a similar way **Archer et al.** (2010) demonstrated how the peer groups of working-class girls reinforced what they described as a **hyper-heterosexual feminine identity**. This was based on looking 'glamorous' and consuming branded sports clothes such as Nike. Girls would be '**policed**' into this identity by their peers and would suffer verbal abuse if they did not conform.

Hegemonic masculinity How males maintain dominant social roles over women and other gender identities.

> **Exam tip**
>
> Be prepared to link factors to different feminist theoretical perspectives. For example, while liberal feminists would argue that policies such as the Equal Pay Act and GIST have been largely successful in bringing about greater equality for females, radical feminists would argue that the education system is still based on patriarchy as it continues to limit females' subject and career choices.

> **Exam tip**
>
> The concept of hyper-heterosexual identity can be applied to an essay on gender and achievement. Girls who adopted this identity would come into conflict with the middle-class habitus of the school which could lead to underachievement. Gender identities could also be applied to a question on gender and subject choice, such as the influence of verbal abuse from peers or pupils picking subjects that conform to a specific gender identity.

> **Exam tip**
>
> Be prepared to discuss the complexity of social processes in schools (e.g. it may be too simplistic to suggest that teacher labelling is the sole factor affecting the achievement of a particular social group). The interplay between class, gender and ethnicity and between internal and external factors needs to be considered when answering a question on educational achievement or identity (and subject choice in terms of gender).

> **Knowledge check 10**
>
> Outline three ways in which gender socialisation may influence subject choice.

> **Summary**
>
> After studying this section, you should be able to explain the differential educational achievement and subject choice of social groups by gender in contemporary society and the relationships and processes within schools relating to gender. You should be familiar with the following:
> - external factors including changes in the family, women's employment and girls' priorities; gender socialisation at home and in society; and the impact of feminism
> - internal factors including processes in schools such as teacher–pupil relationships, labelling, pupil identities and subcultures, the organisation of teaching and learning, the feminisation of education, gender socialisation in school and educational policies

▪ Educational policies

- The 1944 Education Act introduced secondary education for all, with three types of school that were intended to suit three types of intelligence. This tripartite system was **based on selection** — entry to the different types of school (grammar, technical or modern) depended on performance in the 11+ exam. The system drew on the idea that intelligence was fixed at birth, and that the 11+ exam could correctly place children into one of three main intelligence groups.

- While this policy was aimed at **reducing class inequalities**, selection based on the 11+ exam was thought to favour middle-class students. From 1965, the tripartite system was largely replaced by the **comprehensive system**, which was **non-selective** as there was no entry exam. This policy was again aimed at reducing class inequalities as all children were meant to get equal opportunities and attend their local school.

1988 Education Reform Act (ERA)

- The 1988 ERA introduced policies that were influenced by the New Right's view that **marketisation** and **privatisation** of the education system would improve standards, increase competition and make schools more responsive to the needs of the global economy. Policies of parental choice, opting out, formula funding and open enrolment meant a **return to selection** (see page 9).

- A **National Curriculum** of compulsory subjects for all 5- to 16-year-olds was introduced.

- Pupils had to sit national tests (SATs), initially at 7, 11 and 14.

- **League tables** for SATs and GCSEs and **Ofsted reports** were to be published, which parents could use to make an informed choice on where to send their children.

- **City Technology Colleges** (CTCs) were forerunners of academies. They reflected the New Right's drive towards the privatisation of education as they were outside of local authority control, were part-funded by private businesses and had great powers of selection.

New Labour policies (1997–2010)

- New Labour's policies have been described as '**third way**' politics as they included more traditional Labour policies, aimed at **reducing inequality** in achievement, but also incorporated the New Right's emphasis on **diversity and choice** and responding to the needs of the global economy (see Table 6).

- A key policy that continued the New Right's move towards greater **privatisation** in education was the 2000 Learning Skills Act, which introduced **academies**. These City Academies (later called Sponsored Academies) originally required private sponsorship with the aim of bringing 'private sector best practice and innovative management' into failing schools.

- Another proposed policy was raising the participation age to 18. Pupils who left school at 16 would have to continue with some form of education or training. This policy was aimed at addressing inequality by dealing with the increasing number of 'Neets' (those '**n**ot in **e**ducation, **e**mployment or **t**raining') who were mainly from working-class backgrounds.

Exam tip

When answering a question on policies, you may be able to apply policies that relate to reducing inequalities in terms of gender and ethnicity as well as class. For example, GIST was aimed at encouraging greater participation of girls in science and technology, while a range of multicultural and social inclusion policies — such as funding for EAL (English as an additional language) — have been introduced in relation to ethnicity.

- New Labour also continued the New Right's emphasis on promoting vocational education and training, particularly for disaffected students.

Table 6 Key New Labour policies

Policies influenced by the New Right	Policies aimed at reducing inequality
Establishing specialist schools that would give greater choice to parents	Sure Start programmes (including nursery schools) aimed at tackling social exclusion
Encouraging faith schools which were usually set up by single-faith groups	Education Action Zones — meant additional funding in areas of high social deprivation
Sponsored Academies — aimed at raising achievement through greater competition as well as providing greater choice	Education Maintenance Allowance (EMA) — encouraged children from low-income families to stay on in education at 16
Introducing tuition fees for higher education — meant that universities would face greater competition in attracting students	Aimhigher — to encourage children from low-income families to aspire to go on to higher education

Conservative–Liberal Democrat coalition government 2010–15 and beyond

- Under the 2010 Academies Act, the government invited all secondary schools to become '**Converter Academies**', which meant that schools would opt out of local authority control and receive all of their funding direct from government, with the option of buying services at a cheaper rate.
- The Act also introduced new academies, **Free Schools**, set up by 'founding groups' which included parents, education charities, businesses and religious groups.
- In 2012 the academy scheme was extended to primary schools.
- New Labour policies on reducing inequality were either scrapped, as in the case of EMA, or greatly reduced, as in the case of Sure Start provision. Also, tuition fees (in England and Wales) were increased from £3,000 to a maximum of £9,000 per year.
- The **raising of the participation age** was introduced in two stages. Pupils who left Year 11 in the summer of 2014 or later had to continue with some form of education or training at least until their eighteenth birthday. If the education or training was part-time, it had to be combined with at least 20 hours of employment or voluntary work.
- However, policies to reduce inequality were also introduced. The **Pupil Premium** in 2011 gave schools additional funding for each pupil from a disadvantaged background. In 2014–15 the Pupil Premium Plus meant schools received £1,900 for children who were looked after (in local authority care).
- The Conservative governments of Cameron, May and Johnson since 2015 have continued the emphasis on the marketisation of education by making it quicker and easier for schools to convert to academies and by funding the expansion of grammar schools.

Exam tip

As well as trying to standardise assessments, the National Curriculum has had the knock-on effect of improving the achievement of girls in subjects like science which they could no longer opt out of. Having studied science subjects for GCSE, girls were also more likely to opt for them post-16, so subject choice has also been impacted.

Globalisation, privatisation and education policies

- An inevitable consequence of **marketisation** policies has been an increase in the **privatisation** of the education system. By 2019, nearly three quarters of students in England and Wales attended secondary schools that had converted to academies or were free schools and were therefore out of local authority control.
- Another example of the reduced role of local authorities has been the increased level of privatisation of educational services such as specialist behaviour and learning support.
- The New Labour policy of encouraging public–private partnerships (PPPs) facilitated the increasing involvement of private companies in the financing and building of state schools.
- Postmodernists (see page 10) would argue that recent policies promoting diversity and choice have allowed schools to be more flexible and better able to adapt to the changes faced in a postmodern society. For example, **globalisation** has led to an increase in numbers of migrant workers in the UK and schools have been able to respond to this by buying in additional EAL support for the increasing number of students whose first language is not English.
- Postmodernists would argue that schools and other educational institutions are now responding to the demands of a **post-Fordist** economy that has developed as a result of globalisation. For example, schools are offering personalised timetables and there has been an increase in more flexible approaches to education such as distance learning via the internet and lifelong learning.
- The global nature of privatisation in the education system is illustrated by the growth of international education management organisations such as EdisonLearning Inc. in the UK. This company based in the USA claims to be able to improve student achievement while making a profit for its shareholders.

Exam tip

You should be able to relate sociological theory to the impact that these policies may have on inequality in achievement. For example, a school with falling rolls and less funding will be less able to afford to buy in services such as specialist learning and behaviour support. Marxists would argue that these are the very schools that need such support because they are in deprived areas and are less able to select high-achieving students.

Knowledge check 11

Outline two ways in which education has become more privatised.

Evaluation

- + Schools have become more accountable to parents as a result of New Right-influenced marketisation policies. The publication of Ofsted reports and league tables has provided parents with more information about school performance.
- + There is some evidence to suggest that some academies have improved the performance of the struggling inner-city schools that they replaced.
- + Postmodernists would support New Labour's promotion of lifelong learning as it enables adults to retrain to gain the skills required for the ever-changing needs of the economy.
- + New Labour did invest more money in education and had a range of policies aimed at reducing inequality, such as Education Action Zones.
- – Marxists would argue that New Labour policies may have had little impact on tackling structural inequalities in society in relation to both class and ethnic differences.
- – It has been argued that there is a contradiction in New Labour policies. EMA and Aimhigher encouraged students from lower-income families to go into higher education, but New Labour also introduced tuition fees, which may have discouraged such students from going to university because of concerns about repayment.

- ■ – As with compensatory policies such as Operation Head Start in the USA, New Labour's Sure Start programme has been accused of being patronising to the working class as it implies that their values are inferior and that they need help to be 'good parents'.
- ■ – New Right policies of marketisation and parentocracy, continued to some extent by New Labour, have been accused of favouring the middle class (see page 9).

Summary

After studying this section, you should be able to explain the significance of educational policies. You should be familiar with the following:
- ■ policies aimed at achieving greater equality of opportunity of outcome and access to education
- ■ the impact of sociological theory and globalisation on educational policy
- ■ policies of selection, marketisation and privatisation

■ Sociological research methods

Types of methods and data

Sociologists can use either **primary methods**, where the information is collected by the researchers themselves, or **secondary methods**, where the information is gathered by someone else. With primary methods, sociologists can gather the precise data they need, whereas existing data from secondary sources may not provide exactly what the sociologist requires. Data can also be divided into **quantitative**, which is in numerical form, or **qualitative**, which gives a detailed picture of people's opinions and meanings.

Factors that influence choice of method

Theoretical issues

There are three key concepts that relate to theoretical issues:
- ■ **Validity** refers to whether a method measures what it sets out to measure. Valid data is in-depth and will give a 'true picture' of reality.
- ■ **Reliability** refers to whether a method can be repeated or **replicated**. Research is reliable if other sociologists using the same methods get the same results.
- ■ **Representativeness** refers to whether the group studied is a true cross section of the population. If the sample used is **representative**, sociologists can **generalise** the findings to the wider population.

There is a close relationship between these three concepts, the types of data and methods sociologists use and sociologists' **methodological perspectives** and **theoretical perspectives**. This can be seen in Figure 1, which shows the contrasts between **positivist** and **interpretivist** methodological perspectives.

Exam tip

You should be able to compare the different types of data and methods. For example, while there is a lack of control with data from secondary methods, primary methods are more expensive and time-consuming.

Methodological perspective The sociologist's view of how the world should be studied. The two contrasting views are positivism and interpretivism.

Theoretical perspective The sociologist's view of the world. The main theories are Marxism, functionalism, interactionism and feminism. For more detail see the section on sociological theory (page 42).

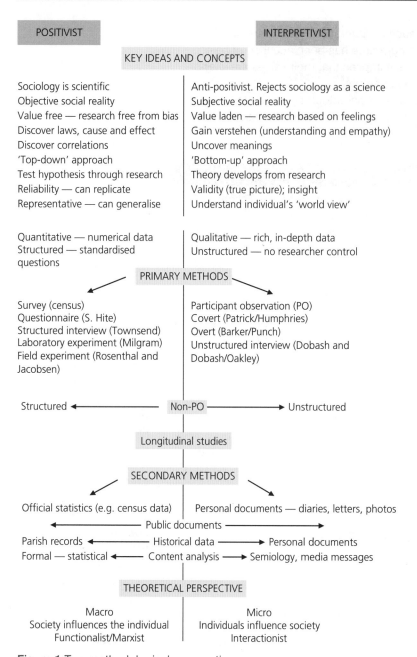

POSITIVIST	INTERPRETIVIST
KEY IDEAS AND CONCEPTS	
Sociology is scientific	Anti-positivist. Rejects sociology as a science
Objective social reality	Subjective social reality
Value free — research free from bias	Value laden — research based on feelings
Discover laws, cause and effect	Gain verstehen (understanding and empathy)
Discover correlations	Uncover meanings
'Top-down' approach	'Bottom-up' approach
Test hypothesis through research	Theory develops from research
Reliability — can replicate	Validity (true picture); insight
Representative — can generalise	Understand individual's 'world view'
Quantitative — numerical data	Qualitative — rich, in-depth data
Structured — standardised questions	Unstructured — no researcher control

PRIMARY METHODS

Survey (census)	Participant observation (PO)
Questionnaire (S. Hite)	Covert (Patrick/Humphries)
Structured interview (Townsend)	Overt (Barker/Punch)
Laboratory experiment (Milgram)	Unstructured interview (Dobash and
Field experiment (Rosenthal and Jacobsen)	Dobash/Oakley)

Structured ◄——————— Non-PO ———————► Unstructured

Longitudinal studies

SECONDARY METHODS

Official statistics (e.g. census data)　　Personal documents — diaries, letters, photos

◄——————— Public documents ———————►

Parish records ◄——— Historical data ———► Personal documents

Formal — statistical ◄——— Content analysis ———► Semiology, media messages

THEORETICAL PERSPECTIVE

Macro	Micro
Society influences the individual	Individuals influence society
Functionalist/Marxist	Interactionist

Figure 1 Two methodological perspectives

While Figure 1 provides a useful outline of the link between theory and method, it is to a certain extent artificial, as researchers' choice of method may be influenced by a variety of factors, including practical and ethical issues. For example, consider a researcher carrying out a **longitudinal study**. Rather than being a specific type of method, this is a study where the researcher follows the same sample over an extended period and conducts research at set intervals (e.g. every five years). Within this type of study, a positivist would favour the use of questionnaires to gain statistics so correlations over time could be measured and causes identified.

In an essay you should state that sociologists who take a particular methodological perspective would *prefer to use* certain methods. Practical or ethical issues could have a greater influence. An interactionist may prefer to use an interpretivist method to study working-class underachievement, but the government may only be willing to fund a method that produces quantitative data.

In contrast, an interpretivist would value longitudinal research for providing more than just a one-off snapshot and would favour the use of unstructured interviews to examine developments over time. However, for both types of approach a researcher would face some practical problems of longitudinal research. It is costly, takes time to get results and faces sample attrition — people may drop out of the study, so the sample may become less representative.

Positivism versus interpretivism

- **Positivists** see behaviour as being determined by external forces beyond the individual's control. **Interpretivists** argue that individuals make sense of situations during social interactions.
- **Positivists** argue that these external forces, called **social facts**, should be studied scientifically. **Interpretivists** argue that sociologists can only study the meanings that individuals give to their behaviour by using **verstehen**.
- **Positivists** use methods that produce quantitative data to examine cause and effect and make laws about human behaviour. **Interpretivists** use methods that produce qualitative data in order to understand behaviour from the individual's point of view and gain insight.

Practical issues

- **Time** Some methods are more time-consuming than others. With covert participant observation, it can often take months for an individual researcher just to gain entry and be accepted by the group studied. In comparison, a self-complete questionnaire can be posted or emailed to respondents by a team of researchers relatively quickly.
- **Cost** Methods using secondary data such as official statistics are often free as these are in the public domain, whereas unstructured interviews are a relatively expensive method due to the costs of training interviewers. Cost relates to time, as the money available affects issues such as how long can be spent on a particular method or sample size. Only the government can afford to conduct a large-scale survey like the census, whereas an individual researcher could conduct a small group interview relatively quickly and cheaply.
- **Funding** Funding bodies such as the government usually require quantitative data in order to gain statistical evidence to measure the impact of educational policies, for example. The sociologist therefore may have no choice but to use methods such as questionnaires or structured interviews. For large-scale research, financial backing from funding bodies is often the most important influence on choice of method.
- **Personal characteristics and skills of the researcher** Some methods, such as covert participant observation and unstructured interviews, require considerable interpersonal skill in order to develop a **rapport** with those studied. Some researchers may prefer to avoid the dangerous situations that can arise from covert research. It would also be difficult for a female to conduct a participant observation study on topics such as homosexual activities in male toilets (Humphries) or football hooliganism.
- **Access and opportunity** Access to conduct interviews within organisations like schools can be denied by **gatekeepers** such as head teachers. This may restrict a researcher to using a postal questionnaire or secondary methods. Barker was invited by the Moonies to study them and so was able to use observation, interviews and questionnaires in her research (**triangulation**).

Social facts These are things that exist externally to the individual, which the individual cannot control. This concept was developed by Durkheim (1895) who felt that positivist methods should be used to study social facts like suicide.

Verstehen This refers to understanding social action via placing oneself in someone else's position (empathy). This concept was developed by Max Weber (1922) as a critical response to positivist sociology.

Exam tip

In an essay, discuss how sociologists may also decide to triangulate and use more than one type of method. For example, Dobash and Dobash studied domestic violence using both structured interviews (to gather statistics on injuries) and unstructured interviews (to gain insight into experiences).

Rapport A relationship of trust which, if achieved, can lead to a researcher gaining valid data.

Triangulation Combining different research methods or sources of data to get a more 'rounded picture' of social reality.

Ethical issues

Sociologists should follow **ethical guidelines** as laid out by the British Sociological Association.

- **Informed consent** Consent is when the participants have agreed to take part in research. In order to gain informed consent, the researcher needs to ensure that participants also know the purpose of the research.
- **Right to withdraw** Once they have agreed to take part, participants should be able to drop out at any time.
- **Deception** The issue of deception may arise. For example, in covert participant observation the researcher will usually have to lie to the group in order to gain access. Researchers need to deal with this issue, for example by debriefing participants on the purpose of the research when it has been completed.
- **Harm** Researchers must ensure that participants do not suffer any physical or mental harm as a result of the research.
- **Confidentiality** The personal details and identities of participants must remain confidential. Consider, for example, Humphries' study of homosexual activities in male toilets (see page 37) — if the men's identities had been revealed, it could have had a devastating impact on their lives.

Importance of these factors

Perhaps the biggest influence on a sociologist's choice of method is their methodological and theoretical perspective. Marxists are more likely to use positivist methods as they help to give a large-scale, 'macro' view of patterns of behaviour in society. For Marxists, quantitative data such as statistics from social surveys on poverty will provide evidence of what they would argue are patterns of inequality in a capitalist society. As interactionists are more interested in gaining verstehen, they are more likely to use interpretivist methods to obtain a small-scale, micro view of patterns of behaviour. For example, interactionists will use research methods such as unstructured interviews or observation to examine interaction between teachers and pupils in relation to issues such as teacher labelling.

However, practical and ethical factors can also have a major influence on a sociologist's choice of method. These factors may restrict the choice regardless of the sociologist's methodological or theoretical perspective.

Factors that influence choice of topic

Theoretical perspective

The major concerns of different sociological theories will inevitably influence choice of topic. Marxist sociologists are likely to choose issues that reflect what they feel are the inevitable consequences of a capitalist system, such as income inequality between the classes, while feminists are likely to choose issues such as the reasons for the pay gap between males and females.

Exam tip

A good form of evaluation is to discuss strategies that a researcher may use to deal with ethical issues such as lack of consent. If deception is used, sociologists can **debrief** participants on the purpose of the research when it has been completed.

Exam tip

Be prepared to discuss how PET (practical, ethical and theoretical) factors are connected. The theoretical advantage of gaining valid data from a method often comes with practical problems of time and cost. For example, rapport can take a long time to build in covert participant observation or unstructured interviews.

Exam tip

Many points on factors affecting choice of topic (theoretical and practical) are similar to points on factors that affect choice of method. While exam questions tend to focus on choice of method, make sure you are able to apply these points to choice of topic. You may be asked to look at both!

Practical issues

- **Access** Some topics such as corporate crime may be difficult to study due to their secretive nature.
- **Funding** Organisations funding research will favour topics they feel are important. Governments are inclined to fund research on topics that interest them for political reasons.
- **Opportunity** Barker had the unusual opportunity to study a religious cult after being invited by the Moonies to study them.

Contemporary issues

Sociologists, like anyone else, will be influenced by and interested in the issues of the day. They are likely to study topics that are being widely covered in the media at the time.

Summary

After studying this section, you should be able to explain:
- the distinction between primary and secondary data, and between quantitative and qualitative data
- the relationship between positivism, interpretivism and sociological methods; the nature of 'social facts'
- the relationship between sociological theory and methods
- the theoretical, practical and ethical considerations influencing choice of topic and choice of methods, and how these are interrelated

---

Primary research

Conducting a survey

The commonest way to gather data is to conduct a social survey using a self-complete questionnaire or interview. Social surveys have practical advantages as large amounts of quantitative data can be gathered relatively quickly using **pre-coded questions**. Once the sociologist has chosen their topic and acquired funding, various steps need to be undertaken before the research can be conducted. First a research question or aim will need to be formulated, which will narrow the focus of the research. For example, a survey might aim to examine the reasons for differential gender achievement. After establishing an aim, a sociologist may then wish to test a specific **hypothesis**. For example, a survey on gender and achievement might test the following hypothesis: 'Gender differences in achievement are the result of differences in teacher attention.'

Before a hypothesis can be tested, concepts need to be operationalised — that is, clearly defined and made measurable. For example, 'teacher attention' could be operationalised in terms of how often a student is asked a question by a teacher. Finally, before the survey is undertaken, the researcher should conduct a pilot study or 'test run' of the draft questionnaire or **interview schedule** to check whether the questions are clearly understood.

Sampling

For practical reasons sociologists cannot study all of the **research population**, so a sample has to be used.

Pre-coded questions Where each possible response to a question is given a code so that the researcher (for an interview) or respondent (for a self-complete questionnaire) can simply circle the number which corresponds to the chosen answer. This allows data to be quickly analysed via a computer.

Hypothesis A statement which offers an explanation which is tested.

Interview schedule A list of the interview questions.

Research population The whole group the researcher is interested in studying.

Representative sampling

Sociologists, particularly positivists, will usually use a sample that is representative and reflects a cross section of the research population in order that they can generalise their findings. In the above example of gender and achievement, the research population is the 1,000 pupils at a school and the researcher could use the following techniques to obtain the desired sample of 100.

- **Simple random sampling** This is where everyone has an equal chance of being selected. In the example, the sample would be the first 100 student names drawn out of a hat.
- **Systematic random sampling** This involves picking every 'nth' number from a sampling frame, which is a list of names of those in the research population. In the example, this would mean picking every tenth pupil from the school's roll. As with random sampling, it is unlikely that the sample produced would be representative (e.g. that 50 females and 50 males would be selected).
- **Stratified random sampling** This involves dividing the research population into specific groups and making a random selection with the right proportions. If the researcher stratified by age and gender in the school survey, it would mean that ten males and ten females from each of Years 7 to 11 would be randomly selected to make up the sample of 100.
- **Quota sampling** This involves the researcher picking people for the sample who fit a certain category. This is non-random as the researcher chooses each person but, like stratified random sampling, it can lead to a representative sample. In the example, the researcher could decide to have a quota of two males and two females from minority ethnic backgrounds among the ten students in each year group (if this was proportional to the population of the school).

Non-representative sampling methods

However, sociologists, particularly interpretivists, may not be interested in generalising and so may use a non-representative sample. There may also be practical reasons why a representative sample cannot be obtained. For example, there is no sampling frame for criminals, who are also likely to refuse to take part in a survey. For such groups **snowball sampling** can be used, where an initial contact gives more names for the sample. One criminal might put the researcher in contact with two more criminals, for example, and so the sample would increase (snowball). **Opportunity sampling** such as interviewing people in a shopping centre may be practical but is also not intended to be representative.

For the following sociological research methods, WWWE (**W**hat, **W**ho and **W**hy, and **E**valuation) is used to define and outline their major strengths and weaknesses. The first evaluation point refers to why positivists or interpretivists would not use the method. Where subsequent points are numbered, strengths (+) of the method have been related to weaknesses (−). Other evaluation points or tables may follow.

Questionnaires

What A questionnaire is a list of standardised questions, usually closed, with pre-coded answers. Self-complete questionnaires are usually sent to respondents' homes and returned by post or email but they can be distributed in person (e.g. in

Knowledge check 12

Outline two types of random sampling techniques.

a classroom). If a questionnaire is read out to a respondent this becomes a structured interview (see page 34).

Who and **Why** Positivists would tend to use questionnaires as, due to their standardised nature, they are reliable and provide quantitative data which can be used to establish correlations and test a hypothesis.

Evaluation

However, interpretivists would reject questionnaires as they do not give a true picture of respondents' meanings and so lack validity.

1 + They can be distributed to a large, geographically spread (P) and representative sample (T).

   – They may be seen as 'junk mail' or 'spam' and only certain people may return them, leading to a low response rate (P) and potentially an unrepresentative sample (T).

2 + They are quick and cheap (P).

   – They may take a long time to be returned and an incentive (such as a free pen) may be needed to get respondents to fill in and complete them, which will add to the cost (P).

3 + As they are self-complete, there are no interviewer costs (P) or **interviewer bias** (T).

   – There is no control for the researcher; the respondent may not receive the questionnaire or the wrong person may fill it in. The questions cannot be explained (P).

4 + Closed, pre-coded questions are easy to analyse via computer programs so patterns and correlations can be identified (P).

   – The **imposition problem** may undermine validity (T) as respondents may not be able to express their true feelings in closed questions (P).

5 + Detachment: positivists favour questionnaires as they are objective — there is no personal contact between the researcher and the respondent (T).

   – Detachment: interpretivists reject questionnaires as a lack of contact leads to a lack of verstehen — meanings cannot be clarified by the researcher (T).

6 + There are relatively few ethical issues due to the lack of contact (E).

   – A researcher still needs to gain informed consent, ensure anonymity and not use questions that may lead to harm (E).

Studies

- **Shere Hite** (1991). This study illustrates that questionnaires may not be appropriate for studying certain topics, in this case women's sexual health. As the questions related to sensitive and personal issues, there was a low response rate (4.5%) meaning that findings could not be generalised due to the sample being unrepresentative. Only certain types of women may have responded.

Exam tip

WWWE can be used as a template for your introduction for a Methods in Context question or a 20-mark methods essay question for Paper 3. In essays you should try to link strengths of a method to weaknesses based on **p**ractical, **e**thical and **t**heoretical issues (PET). You should also use examples and studies to develop AO2 and AO3.

Interviewer bias
Where an interviewer affects the respondent's answers and thereby reduces validity, for example through tone of voice, facial expressions or, particularly in unstructured interviews, leading questions.

Imposition problem
Where a researcher 'forces' the respondent to answer in a certain way; for example, with closed questions and pre-coded responses, the researcher has already decided what questions are important and how people can respond.

■ **Bowles and Gintis** (1976). Bowles and Gintis gave 237 questionnaires to New York high school students to gain information on the character traits that were rewarded by schools and employers. They used a reasonably large sample so that they could generalise their findings and support their hypothesis that the correspondence principle existed between schools and the workplace.

Knowledge check 13

Outline two theoretical strengths of using questionnaires.

Structured interviews

What A structured interview is when a questionnaire (a list of standardised questions, usually closed, with pre-coded answers) is read out to respondents and filled in by a trained interviewer.

Who and **Why** Positivists would tend to use structured interviews as, due to their standardised nature, they are reliable. They provide quantitative data which can be used to establish correlations and test a hypothesis.

Evaluation

However, interpretivists reject structured interviews as they do not give a true picture of respondents' meanings and so lack validity.

Structured interviews share the main strengths and weaknesses of questionnaires. Table 7 shows the advantages and disadvantages of structured interviews in comparison to questionnaires.

Table 7 Advantages and disadvantages of structured interviews compared to questionnaires

Advantages	Disadvantages
Higher response rate as respondents find it harder to turn down a researcher if face to face (P)	They are more expensive due to interviewer costs and cannot have as geographically dispersed and as large samples (P)
It is more difficult for a respondent to lie face to face so potentially data are more valid (T)	Respondents are more likely to give socially desirable answers due to wanting to show themselves in a good light (T)
Interviewers can clarify questions, although they may have strict guidelines to follow (T)	Interviewer bias may undermine validity (T)

Studies

■ **Young and Willmott** (1962). This study used structured interviews to gather large amounts of factual data about family life in London. The study also illustrates the practical advantages of having a large sample (987 people) and having a high response rate (94%).
■ **Peter Townsend** (1979). This study used structured interviews to administer a 39-page questionnaire on poverty in the UK. As well as having a high response rate (76%) to a large sample (2,052 people), interviewers were required to administer pre-coded questions on household income that were often complex.

Unstructured interviews

What An unstructured interview is an informal conversation between an interviewer and a respondent which has no set format.

Who and **Why** Interpretivists would tend to use unstructured interviews as they enable respondents to discuss issues from their point of view, allowing the researcher to gain verstehen and valid data.

Evaluation

However, positivists reject unstructured interviews as they are non-standardised and so data gained will lack reliability. As samples are usually small, they are likely to be unrepresentative.

1 + The freedom of having no structure and open questions allows the researcher to follow up leads (P).

   − They can be time-consuming and expensive. Responses will be difficult to quantify and may be irrelevant (P).

2 + If a rapport is developed (P), valid data can be obtained on sensitive topics (T).

   − This will only occur if the researcher is highly skilled (P), and rapport may lead to socially desirable responses (T).

3 + They enable the researcher to uncover the meanings behind the respondent's actions without the imposition problem (T).

   − The problem of interview bias is greater than with structured interviews; for example, interviewers may only follow up leads they feel are important (T).

4 + There are relatively few ethical issues as consent is obtained (E).

   − The interviewee may feel under pressure to answer questions that are personal. The right to withdraw and anonymity must be ensured (E).

Exam tip

Be prepared to relate methods to theory. For example, feminists are in favour of unstructured interviews as they allow women to be more in control of the research process.

Interviews can also be **semi-structured**, which is when there are some structured, more standardised questions but the interviewer is allowed the flexibility to follow up areas of interest. Sociologists can also conduct **group interviews** with respondents, who are sometimes called **focus groups**. The advantages of these are that groups, such as students, may be more relaxed and can 'bounce ideas off' one another, leading to more valid data. However, there are also problems: one member of the group may dominate the discussion and peer pressure may affect the validity of responses. Interpretivists prefer these methods as valid data can be obtained. However, positivists would argue that their non-standardised nature leads to a lack of reliability.

Focus group An informal group interview where a researcher introduces a topic and allows the group to tease out responses from one another.

Studies

■ **Dobash and Dobash** (1980). Dobash and Dobash conducted 109 unstructured interviews with women who had been the victims of domestic violence. To help gain rapport on this very sensitive issue, the interviews were conducted informally in the refuges where the women lived. The interviews gained valid data but raised practical problems as they took between 2 and 12 hours.

■ **Ann Oakley** (1973). Oakley interviewed 66 women during and after pregnancy. The study illustrates that if the interviewer gains empathy and rapport with the interviewees they will feel comfortable discussing personal subjects. A possible theoretical problem is that Oakley may have become too attached to the women so the data may have lacked validity.

Participant observation (PO)

What Where the researcher joins in with the activities of the group being studied. This can be either **covert**, where the researcher goes 'undercover' ('closed') or **overt**, where the researcher's true identity is made known ('open').

Who and **Why** Interpretivists would tend to use PO as it gives a first-hand insight into the social interactions and behaviour of the group studied.

Evaluation

However, positivists would reject PO due to its lack of reliability as it cannot be standardised or replicated. Tables 8, 9 and 10 constitute a 'revision chart' for PO that could be used for other methods.

Table 8 Strengths and weaknesses of both covert and overt PO

Strengths	Weaknesses
Can observe people in their natural setting and gain valid data (T)	Can only observe small groups, so cannot generalise findings (P)
Subjective involvement means insight and verstehen can be gained (T)	Positivists argue that PO is not scientific. As it is based on one researcher's interpretation it cannot be replicated (T)
Can study behaviour of groups over time (P)	PO can be time-consuming and expensive (P)

Table 9 Comparison of covert and overt PO

Covert	Overt
Lack of informed consent (E)	Honest method as there is no deception (E)
Hawthorne effect does not occur but the presence of the researcher may still affect the group dynamics (T)	Hawthorne effect means data may lack validity. Behaviour will change if participants know they are being observed (T)
Asking certain questions openly may blow the researcher's cover (P)	Can ask naive but important questions and use other methods openly (P)
Will have to record information later (P) and rely on memory, which may affect validity (T)	Easy to record information (P)
Researcher may have to take part in activities they disagree with or break the law (P) (E)	Researcher does not have to take part in all the group's activities as they are not 'one of them' (P) (E)

Table 10 Covert and overt PO in relation to 'getting in, staying in and getting out'

Covert	Overt
Getting in Hard to gain access, particularly with deviant groups	With overt, the group may deny access or stop the researcher from seeing everything.
Staying in Researcher may 'go native' and get too involved	With overt, the researcher is less likely to 'go native'
Getting out Leaving the group may be difficult	Less of a problem for overt as the researcher is not pretending to be part of the group

Exam tip

For an essay on methods, you should be prepared to compare the strengths of the method stated in the question with other methods, as is done with overt and covert PO in the tables.

Hawthorne effect

When people change their behaviour because they know that they are being observed.

When conducting participant observation, sociologists sometimes fall between being covert and being overt. Studies such as Patrick can be described as **semi-overt** as a key member of the group, such as a gang leader, is told the real purpose of the study. William Foote Whyte (1938) told the gang that the reason for joining was that he needed information for a book he was writing about their neighbourhood. Only the gang leader was told it was actually the gang itself he was studying.

Although less common, sociologists can also use covert and overt non-participant observation. Interpretivists would tend not to use this method as they would argue that a lack of participation in the activities of the group reduces the level of verstehen and therefore validity. While positivists totally reject participant observation, they may occasionally use non-participant observation using a **structured observation schedule**. For example, in a lesson observation the frequency of interactions between teachers and pupils could be quantified and used to establish correlations.

Studies

- **James Patrick** (1973). Patrick's **covert** study of a Glasgow gang illustrates the issue of 'getting in' as he was close to the boys' age and gained access through the gang leader, 'Tim'. 'Getting out' was a problem for Patrick as he had to leave the gang abruptly due to the violence. Fearing repercussions, he published his study years later under a false name.

- **Laud Humphries** (1970). Humphries' initially **covert** study of gay sexual activities in public toilets in the USA illustrates the issue of 'getting in' in terms of the observer's role. Humphries acted as a 'watch queen' (lookout) to help him gain the trust of this very secretive group who were engaging in illegal behaviour. Once he had gained their trust, Humphries revealed the purpose of his research to certain participants (became **overt**), which allowed him to use other methods such as interviews.

- **Maurice Punch** (1979). Punch's **overt** study of Amsterdam police illustrates the problem of 'getting in' as the police officers only let Punch see certain aspects of their activities on patrol. It also shows the issue of 'staying in' in terms of going native as he started behaving like a police officer and chased suspects.

- **Eileen Barker** (1984). Barker's **case study** on a religious sect (the Moonies) and whether they were 'brainwashing' their members shows how a researcher conducting **overt** participant observation can become a 'trusted outsider'. While initially her observations may have lacked validity due to the Hawthorne effect, Barker was with the Moonies for 6 years and was able to build up rapport with group members. Barker may have 'gone native', however, and become too sympathetic to the Moonies, compromising the validity of her findings. Was Barker herself brainwashed by the Moonies?

Laboratory experiments

What A laboratory experiment is a test carried out in a controlled environment to establish cause and effect between identified variables. The researcher changes the independent variable to measure the effect on the dependent variable.

Who and **Why** Positivists tend to use laboratory experiments as, due to their high levels of reliability, they are easy to replicate.

Structured observation schedule A predefined list of behaviour patterns that a researcher is investigating.

Case study A detailed study of one group or event, usually involving a variety of qualitative methods. Barker used overt observation, questionnaires and unstructured interviews in her study on the Moonies. While interpretivists favour case studies due to valid data being gained, positivists would reject their use as the findings cannot be generalised.

Exam tip

If a question asks you to evaluate the problems of using covert or overt participant observation, be prepared to use non-participant observation as evaluation to compare the relative strengths and weaknesses of the methods.

Knowledge check 14

Outline two ethical problems of using covert participant observation.

Evaluation

However, interpretivists reject their use as they lack **ecological validity** due to the fact that they take place in an artificial environment.

1   + As the researcher has control over the experiment (P), the data should be reliable (T).

      – The variables that influence human behaviour cannot easily be identified or controlled (P).

2   +Behaviour patterns can be measured quantitatively via manipulating variables (P).

      – The behaviour of the participant could be influenced by the Hawthorne effect and **experimenter effect** rather than by the independent variable (T).

Other problems:

- Ethical issues — laboratory experiments often involve deception as to the true purpose of the experiment and may cause emotional or even physical harm to the participants (E).
- They cannot be used to study the past (P).
- They are not representative (T) due to their small scale (P).

Ecological validity
This means that the method and setting of the study can be applied to everyday life.

Experimenter effect
When the behaviour of a participant is influenced by their awareness that they are involved in an experiment.

> **Exam tip**
>
> In an essay, develop analysis by stating that due to these problems even positivists are unlikely to use laboratory experiments despite their high reliability.

Studies

- **Stanley Milgram** (1974). In this 'shocking' study, participants were misled into thinking that they were administering potentially fatal electric shocks to people when they answered a question incorrectly. Despite the ethical problems of deception, physical harm (some had seizures) and emotional harm (knowing that they could have killed because they were told to), Milgram's study illustrates the argument that 'the end justifies the means'. In the debrief, 74% of participants felt they had learned something on Milgram's topic of obedience and authority, despite being deceived.

- **Albert Bandura** (1961). Bandura's experiment on the influence of the media on violent behaviour illustrates the ethical issues of whether children can give their full informed consent and the potential harm caused by the researcher exposing them to violence. In terms of practical issues, Bandura may not have been able to control variables such as the amount of violence children may have experienced at home. The study also lacks ecological validity because the children were not playing in a natural environment.

Knowledge check 15

Outline two practical problems of using laboratory experiments.

Field experiments

What A field experiment is a test carried out in a natural environment to establish cause and effect between identified variables.

Who and **Why** Positivists could potentially use field experiments to establish cause and effect to test a hypothesis.

Exam tip

A common error is to confuse field experiments with participant observation. While they may both involve studying a group in their natural environment, in a field experiment the researcher does not participate in the behaviour of the group.

Evaluation

However, despite being able to look at correlations, positivists would argue that, as they have less control over variables, field experiments lack reliability. While field experiments take place in a natural setting, interpretivists reject them as they do not uncover meanings behind actions.

1   + As the research takes place in the participant's natural surroundings, the data will be more valid than in laboratory experiments (T).

   – Variables cannot easily be controlled as is the case in a laboratory (P).

2   + As the participants are usually unaware that they are in an experiment, there is no Hawthorne effect (T).

   – This creates problems of lack of informed consent and deception, which may lead to harm (E).

Studies

- **Rosenthal and Jacobsen** (1968). Rosenthal and Jacobsen conducted a field experiment to test their theory on the self-fulfilling prophecy and the impact of teacher labelling. This study illustrates the problem of identifying and controlling variables. There may have been factors other than the variable of teacher expectations that influenced the improvements in the IQ of the students. It also illustrates ethical problems of deception (as the teachers were lied to) and potential harm (the possible impact on the students' education).
- **Mary Sissons** (1971). Sissons studied the effect of social class on people's willingness to give directions to an actor (who dressed as a businessman then as a labourer outside Paddington train station). This study illustrates the problem of lack of reliability. It would be impossible to have exactly the same members of the public involved, so the study cannot be replicated.

Secondary research

Official statistics

What Official statistics are quantitative data gathered and used by the government and other official bodies.

Who and **Why** Positivists would tend to use official statistics as they are reliable and they can be used to identify correlations to test a hypothesis.

Evaluation

However, interpretivists reject official statistics as they lack validity.

Exam tip

In an essay question, you can develop AO2 and AO3 despite there being no ethical weaknesses of official statistics. Compare the ethical strengths of official statistics (e.g. they are secondary data that do not require consent) with other methods such as covert participant observation, which has ethical issues such as deception and potential harm to both the researcher and the group.

Table 11 Strengths and weaknesses of using official statistics

Strengths	Weaknesses
Often the only source of data in a particular area, e.g. the census (P)	Collected by the government so may not be on the topic researched (P)
Free source of large amounts of quantitative data; in the public domain and easily accessible online (P)	They are secondary data and not collected by sociologists themselves, so there is no control over collection (P)
Data are reliable as they are compiled in a standardised way by 'experts', e.g. the census (T)	Not always fully reliable, e.g. mistakes could be made when data are recorded onto or from census forms (T)
Hard statistics allow accurate comparisons between groups. For example, we can compare statistics on social class and divorce rates (T)	Soft statistics may not be very valid as they do not always measure what they are supposed to. For example, the police do not record all crimes (T)
Show trends and patterns over time as they are often collected at regular intervals. For example, can compare the rise in female achievement after policies like GIST (P). Could be used to test a hypothesis (T)	How data are collected may change over time, e.g. unemployment statistics. Thatcher's government changed definitions over 20 times in 1980s (P). Marxists would argue they are manipulated by the government for political reasons (T)
Positivists argue that the quantitative data enable sociologists to identify and accurately measure behaviour patterns and establish cause and effect relationships (T)	Interpretivists would argue that official statistics are socially constructed, 'made up by society'. For example, crime statistics tell us more about police labelling than levels of crime (T)
Usually large scale and are therefore representative. For example, the census covers the whole population as it is compulsory (T)	Some may not be as representative, as they are only based on a sample of the relevant population, e.g. the Crime Survey for England and Wales (T)
No ethical issues. Anonymous and in the public domain (E)	

Studies

- **Durkheim** (1897). Durkheim used **the comparative method** to compare the suicide rates (official statistics) of different European countries. As a positivist, Durkheim felt that he was able to use a scientific approach to prove his hypothesis that the more integrated into society a person was, the less likely they would be to commit suicide.

- **The Crime Survey of England and Wales**. Formerly the British Crime Survey, this is a systematic victim survey that provides crime statistics based on a sample of up to 50,000 people. Positivist researchers would use statistics from this survey to examine patterns and trends in crime.

Documents

What Documents refer to a wide range of written and other 'texts' that can be personal (such as letters, photo albums and autobiographies) or public (such as government reports).

Who and **Why** Interpretivists would tend to use them, particularly personal, expressive documents such as diaries, as they can be used to uncover meanings and are a rich source of qualitative data.

The comparative method A 'thought experiment' conducted in the mind of a sociologist.

Knowledge check 16

What is the difference between hard and soft official statistics?

Evaluation

Positivists tend not to use documents as they lack reliability due to their unstandardised nature. However, positivists may use formal documents such as parish records which contain quantitative data that could be used to establish correlations.

1 + As they are secondary data, documents are often free, quick and easy to collect (P).

   − They may not be specifically on the topic required and some documents may be difficult to access. There may be legal restrictions on the use of some public documents (P).

2 + As they are secondary, there are limited ethical issues (E).

   − Some documents such as diaries will need consent (E).

3 + Personal documents such as diaries are not written with an audience in mind, so can provide a valid and authentic picture of the writer's thoughts and feelings (T).

   − Personal documents may lack validity. For example, diaries may exaggerate personal experiences while autobiographies are likely to be biased towards the writer's view (T).

4 + Historical documents are sometimes the only way of studying the past (P).

   − There may be no way of checking the validity of the original research (P) (T).

Exam tip

Be prepared to apply John Scott's (1990) checklist when assessing documents' authenticity (is it fake?), credibility (is it believable?), representativeness (is it typical?) and meaning (is it understandable?).

Knowledge check 17

Outline two practical strengths of using documents.

Sociologists may use **content analysis** to systematically study the content of documents, particularly the media. **Formal** content analysis is favoured by positivists to count the frequency of predetermined categories such as male or female voiceovers in adverts. Interpretivists would prefer **semiotic** content analysis, which involves examining the themes and underlying meanings in documents, for example the wording used in news reporting. While media sources have the practical advantages of easy access and low cost, there are problems with content analysis. Formal content analysis would be rejected by interpretivists for not examining the meanings behind the frequency, while positivists would reject more qualitative content analysis for being subjective as it is based on the researcher's interpretation of the media message.

Studies

■ **Thomas and Znaniecki** (1919). This classic study on Polish immigrants to the USA shows the high levels of meaning that documents can provide the researcher. Thomas and Znaniecki used a wide range of private documents, such as letters sent home, and public documents, such as newspaper articles. This study also illustrates a practical problem as they had to advertise and pay people to access some of these documents.

■ **The Glasgow University Media Group**. This group has conducted a wide variety of content analysis studies since the 1970s on a range of issues. These studies have been useful in showing the biased nature of news reporting. They arguably also show that bias can occur in the interpretation of media sources when content analysis is being conducted.

Summary

After studying this section, you should be able to explain:

- the stages a sociologist follows when conducting a survey, including sampling techniques
- sources of data, including questionnaires, interviews, participant and non-participant observation, experiments, documents and official statistics
- the distinction between primary and secondary data, and between quantitative and qualitative data

■ Sociological theory and methods

Sociological theory

- Functionalism is a **consensus** theory which argues that society is based on shared values.
- Marxism is a **conflict** theory which argues that we live in a capitalist society in which there is a relationship based on conflict, with the bourgeoisie (the 'bosses') exploiting the proletariat (the 'workers').
- Both functionalism and Marxism are **macro**, large-scale theories that tend to use positivist methods. These approaches are referred to as **structural** theories as society is seen as shaping individuals' behaviour.
- Social action theories reject structural, macro theories and argue that society is constructed through people's interactions and meanings (such as in the labelling process).
- Social action theories such as interactionism are **micro**, small-scale theories that tend to use interpretivist methods. Some neo-Marxists such as Willis have incorporated social action theory and interpretivist methods into their research.
- Feminists argue that other sociological theories are **malestream**, as they largely ignore gender inequality in society. Feminists mainly use interpretivist methods to study issues such as the division of domestic labour and domestic violence.
- Liberal feminists argue that legislation such as the Equal Pay Act is gradually leading to greater equality for women. However, radical feminists argue that society is based on the oppression of women and that only revolutionary change will bring an end to the gender inequality that results from patriarchy.
- Postmodernists argue that 'modern' theories such as functionalism and Marxism are **meta-narratives** ('big stories') that do not hold the 'truth' about society. They are out of date as they are no longer able to explain the diverse and fragmented nature of postmodern society.
- Theories of late modernity agree with postmodernism that society has changed rapidly in recent years but argue that we are still in the modern era.

Knowledge check 18

Outline two qualitative research methods that Willis used to study the 'lads'.

Exam tip

For A-level Paper 1 you only have a 10-mark question on this area (it can also be on sociological methods). For this question you only need to look at two points, for example two arguments for or against a claim such as sociology being a science, or two advantages or disadvantages of a method. Refer to Student Guide 3 for a more detailed coverage of this topic and for examples of 20-mark questions on Theory and methods.

Sociology, science and value freedom

- Positivists such as **Durkheim** argue that sociology can and should model itself on the natural sciences and use quantitative methods to study society objectively.
- Positivists argue that sociologists can discover laws about human behaviour by using the **inductive** method where data is gathered through observation and measurement. The process of **verification** should be used to prove or refute a hypothesis.
- Positivists believe that as sociologists can study social phenomena objectively, value freedom is possible as the researcher's own beliefs will not influence how they conduct their research or interpret their results.
- **Popper** rejected the inductive approach of positivism and argued that scientific knowledge should be based on the process of **falsification** (that it can be proved wrong) rather than verification. Popper felt that while sociology could be scientific as it can produce a hypothesis that can be tested, most sociology is unscientific as it cannot be proved wrong.
- **Kuhn** argues that as sociology does not have a shared paradigm it cannot be considered to be a science.
- **Realists** argue that — like some natural scientists, such as meteorologists — sociologists have to study society in 'open systems' where variables cannot necessarily be controlled and measured. Therefore, realists argue that, although sociology can attempt to be scientific in studying open systems in a neutral way, it cannot be completely value free.
- Interpretivists and social action theorists reject the claim that sociology can be an objective science. For them the purpose of sociological inquiry is to uncover meanings and gain verstehen through qualitative methods, not to establish cause and effect. They would argue that sociologists need to be subjective rather than objective and will inevitably be influenced by their values.
- **Weber** argued that sociologists could not be value free when choosing a research topic and interpreting and applying findings. However, he felt that researchers must be objective and unbiased when carrying out their research.
- Some sociologists, such as Marxists and feminists, argue that value freedom is undesirable and that sociologists should be **value laden**; they should make value judgements and should aim to improve society through sociological research.

Paradigm An assumed way of looking at the world (e.g. assuming that the Earth is flat).

Knowledge check 19

What is the difference between verification and falsification?

Sociology and social policy

Social policies are government policies that attempt to deal with social problems such as educational underachievement, poverty and crime. Social policy has been influenced by sociological perspectives and research in a variety of ways.

- The social democratic perspective had a significant impact on the introduction of the welfare state after the Second World War. Later, **Townsend's** *Poverty in the United Kingdom* made recommendations to the government to change what he felt was an inadequate benefits system.
- New Right researchers such as **Marsland** and his notion of the dependency culture influenced the Conservative governments to cut back on welfare provision in the 1980s. The New Right believe that the state should have a minimal role in people's lives and therefore they criticise most social policy.

Knowledge check 20

Outline three educational policies that have been influenced by the New Right.

■ Feminist theory and research have influenced government policies aimed at addressing gender inequality, such as GIST and the Equal Pay Act.

■ Many Marxists are critical of government social policies and argue that they can be used by the capitalist system to maintain and justify inequality. For example, they would argue that the minimum wage legitimates exploitation in the labour market while giving the impression to the public that governments are acting in the best interests of the low paid. Some Marxists acknowledge that some social policies have benefited the working class, but for Marxists the main function of such policies is to pacify the proletariat to ensure that they do not rebel.

■ Some sociologists believe that their research should feed into social policy. Functionalists would argue that sociologists should provide the state with scientific, objective information on which the state can base its policies.

■ Others, such as **modern positivists**, feel that it is the job of sociologists to investigate social problems, but that it is up to someone else to solve them.

■ Despite the influence of sociological research on social policy, governments may reject findings for a variety of reasons such as cost and their political standpoint.

Summary

After studying this section, you should be aware of:
■ consensus, conflict, structural and social action theories
■ the concepts of modernity and postmodernity in relation to sociological theory
■ the relationship between theory and methods
■ the nature of science and the extent to which sociology can be regarded as scientific
■ debates about subjectivity, objectivity and value freedom
■ the relationship between sociology and social policy

Questions & Answers

▮ How to use this section

After this introduction, this section of the guide contains three test papers on **education, sociological theory and methods** in the style of the questions you can expect in the A-level Paper 1 examination. The content, timing and mark allocation of this paper are shown below.

Each question is followed by a brief analysis of what to watch out for when answering it. The first two papers include both an A-grade response (Student A) and a C-grade response (Student B) to each question, with commentary, while the third paper shows A-grade responses only. The A-grade responses represent one way of achieving an A grade. However, there is no such thing as a perfect essay. An A grade can be achieved in several different ways. The advice below offers some suggestions on how this can be achieved.

The information in this guide can be used for the following exam papers:

Paper 1 Education with theory and methods

The exam paper is allocated 2 hours.

- **Education** Short answers (4- and 6-mark questions) and extended writing (10- and 30-mark questions). 50 marks
- **Methods in context** One extended writing question. 20 marks
- **Theory and methods** Extended writing. 10 marks

Paper 3 Crime and deviance with theory and methods

- **Theory and methods** Extended writing. 20- and 10-mark questions

There is also a 10-mark 'Outline and explain' question on Paper 3 on Theory and methods, so the questions in this guide will be useful practice for this exam as well. The Content Guidance section in this guide, particularly the part on sociological methods, can be used to help prepare for the 20-mark Theory and methods question in this paper (refer to Student Guide 3 for practice papers for this question and more 10-mark questions on Theory and methods).

Examinable skills

AQA Sociology examination papers are designed to test certain defined skills. These skills are expressed as assessment objectives (AOs). There are three AOs and it is important that you know what these are and what you have to be able to do in an exam to show your ability in each. Further guidance on each of the AOs is given below. In practice, many answers to questions, particularly those carrying the higher marks, will contain elements of all three AOs.

Assessment objective 1 (AO1)

Demonstrate knowledge and understanding of:

- **sociological theories, concepts and evidence**
- **sociological research methods**

Your exam answers will have to demonstrate clearly to the examiners that your knowledge is accurate and appropriate to the topic being discussed and that you have a clear understanding of it. It is not enough simply to reproduce knowledge learned by rote. You must be able to use this knowledge in a meaningful way to answer the specific question set. This means that you must be able to select the appropriate knowledge from everything you know and use only the knowledge that is relevant to, and addresses the issues raised by, the question.

Assessment objective 2 (AO2)

Apply sociological theories, concepts, evidence and research methods to a range of issues.

In certain questions in the exam you will be presented with an item — a short paragraph setting the context for the question that is to follow, and providing you with some information to help answer it. You *must* take this relevant information and use (apply) it in your answer. However, 'applying' the material does not mean simply copying it from the item and leaving it to speak for itself. You will need to show your understanding of the material by doing something with it, such as offering a criticism, explaining something about it, linking it to a particular sociological theory or offering another example of what is being stated or suggested. You will therefore be using your own knowledge to add to the information that you have been given and will be *applying* it appropriately to answer the question. (See the specific guidance below on using the item for Q03.)

Assessment objective 3 (AO3)

Analyse and evaluate sociological theories, concepts, evidence and research methods in order to:

- **present arguments**
- **make judgements**
- **draw conclusions**

The skill of *analysis* is shown by breaking something down into its component parts and subjecting them to detailed examination. Analysis is shown by providing answers (depending, of course, on what you are analysing) to questions such as 'who said or who believes this?', 'what does this concept relate to?', 'what does this research method entail?', 'how was this evidence collected?' and so on. The skill of *evaluation* is shown by the ability to identify the strengths and weaknesses or limitations of any sociological material. It is not sufficient, however, simply to list the strengths or limitations of something — you need to say *why* something is considered a strength or otherwise, and sometimes you will need to state *who* claims that this is a strength or weakness. Depending on what you are discussing, you may be able to reach a conclusion about the relative merits or otherwise of something, but remember to base any conclusions on the rational arguments and solid sociological evidence that you have presented in your answer.

Weighting of assessment objectives

In the exam papers, each AO is given a particular weighting, which indicates its relative importance to the overall mark gained.

Table 12 Weighting for A-level examinations

Assessment objective	Paper 1 (approximate %)	Paper 2 (approximate %)	Paper 3 (approximate %)	Overall weighting
AO1	15	13	16	44
AO2	11	11	9	31
AO3	8	9	8	25
Overall	33.33	33.33	33.33	100

Guidance on how to complete each question

Question 01

Outline two...

Here is an example:

Outline two ways in which factors within schools may affect gender differences in achievement (4 marks).

Each point will be rewarded as 2 marks (1 + 1). You **must** link your explanation to the key words in the question. In this example 1 mark will be given for identifying a factor (e.g. the introduction of coursework) and 1 mark for the explanation of how this affects achievement (e.g. that as girls tend to be more organised, they achieve higher than boys in subjects that have coursework).

Question 02

Outline three...

Here is an example:

Outline three ways in which factors outside of school may affect ethnic differences in educational achievement (6 marks).

Each point will be rewarded as 2 marks (1 + 1). You **must** link your explanation to the key words in the question. In this example 1 mark will be given for identifying a factor (e.g. having English as an additional language) and 1 mark for the explanation of how this affects achievement (e.g. EAL pupils may struggle to read textbooks and answer essay questions in subjects like English).

Question 03

Applying material from Item A, analyse two...

Here is an example:

Applying material from Item A, analyse two ways in which the education system might be functional for society (10 marks; see page 72).

Remember you only need two paragraphs. No introduction or conclusion is required.

> **Exam tip**
>
> It may be worth including an extra point for Questions 01 and 02 as the examiner will mark all the responses given and select the best ones. It is advisable to return to these questions and give an additional point if you have completed your answers before the end of the exam.

> **Exam tip**
>
> Be concise on Questions 01 and 02. You can use bullet points and should not need to write more than two sentences.

The first paragraph for this question could be set out as follows:

- First sentence: Quote the 'hook' from the Item and state what the way is. For the question above, the first sentence could be as follows: The first **way** that the education system might be functional for society is that it helps to create a '**value consensus**'.
- AO1: **Explain** — Outline what this means and give some examples to illustrate. For the question above, how the education system instils shared values such as respect.
- AO3: **Analyse** — Unpack this with a discussion of the **way**. For the question above, how the education system fulfils the socialisation function and leads to value consensus according to functionalists such as Durkheim and Parsons.
- AO2: **Apply** — Apply points clearly to the question. For the question above, explain how this **way** is functional for society.
- AO3: **Evaluation** — Include at least one sentence starting with the word 'However'. For this question, the functionalist view that the education system leads to value consensus and that this is positive for society could be evaluated using criticisms from a Marxist or feminist perspective.

> **Exam tip**
>
> In order to gain good application marks for Q03, it is a good strategy to use the exact words in the question in your response (such as 'way', 'reason' or 'effect').

The same structure should be used for paragraph two, which should quote the second hook in Item A (in this question the 'specialised division of labour' — see page 72).

In addition to 'ways', other words typically used in Question 03 are 'reasons' or 'effects' (i.e. 'analyse two reasons' or 'analyse two effects').

Question 04

Applying material from Item B and your own knowledge, evaluate...

Here is an example:

Applying material from Item B and your knowledge, evaluate the view that home factors are the main cause of differences in the educational achievement of different social groups (30 marks; see page 73).

The template on p. 49 could be used to construct your own more detailed plan for this type of item-based essay question.

The main body of this template is useful for a question that focuses on a particular argument, such as the question above on home factors. You must clearly apply other arguments as to how they agree or disagree with it (such as the internal factor of teacher labelling). If the question requires you to assess sociological explanations of an issue, such as the role of education, you should allocate time more equally to the main arguments.

Template 1 Item-based essay question: 30 marks

Introduction: AAA

- **A:** 'As Item A states…' — In your own words, sum up the main points from the first paragraph of the item.
- **A:** Argument 1 — For the essay above, **external** factors (home factors).
- **A:** Argument 2 — For the essay above, **internal** factors (for example: 'However, interactionists would argue that internal factors such as teacher labelling are more important.')

Main body

Paragraphs 1–3 (or more) on Argument 1 — AO2 and AO3 points in each paragraph.

For each paragraph, develop AO2 and AO3 by using the following techniques:
- Use studies and examples to illustrate strengths and weaknesses of the argument.
- Give **specific** evaluation points on arguments, such as supporting evidence being out of date or that it cannot be generalised easily.
- Give evaluation points from different **sociological perspectives** — how they agree/disagree.

Paragraph 4 on Argument 2 — State how it agrees/disagrees with Argument 1. For the essay above, how interactionists would argue that internal factors are more important.

Paragraph 5 on other possible arguments — State how they agree/disagree with Argument 1. For the essay above, how sociologists such as Archer argue that external and internal factors are interrelated.

Conclusion

'Perhaps the main strength of Argument 1 is that it is right to point to the importance of…'

'Perhaps the main weakness of Argument 1, as Argument 2 points out, is that it ignores the impact of…'

Say **something new**. Try not to just recap previous points in the conclusion. For the essay above, a potential new point is how Evans argues that there is an interplay between class, gender and ethnicity when explaining the achievement of any social group.

Depending on the issue in the question, the number of paragraphs devoted to each argument will vary. You should not wait until paragraph 4 to use other theories to evaluate: do this throughout the essay. In the essay above, you should also discuss how internal factors link with external factors throughout the essay.

Question 05

Applying material from Item C and your knowledge of research methods, evaluate the strengths and limitations of using (*method*) **to investigate** (*issue*).

Here is an example:

Applying material from Item C and your knowledge of research methods, evaluate the strengths and limitations of using questionnaires to investigate parental attitudes towards education (20 marks; see page 73).

The following template could be used to construct your own more detailed plan for this type of Methods in context essay question.

Template 2 Methods in context essay: 20 marks

Introduction: WWWE
- **W**hat — define the method.
- **W**ho — would generally use it?
- **W**hy — would they use it?
- **E**valuation — who would not use the method and, briefly, why?

Main body

Paragraph 1:
- Refer to access to the school.
- For primary methods, refer to gatekeepers such head teachers and, once in the school, teachers.
- Develop analysis on these practical issues — e.g. by noting that a DBS (Disclosure and Barring Service) check takes time and money, or that a head teacher may restrict access because of concerns about the findings damaging the school's reputation and affecting its league table position.
- If the question is on a secondary method that is in the public domain (official statistics or public documents), point out that the researcher doesn't face these practical issues of access.
- Try to apply all these points to the issue and method named in the question.

Remaining paragraphs — Write as many as you can!

Dos
- Apply a particular strength or limitation of the method to the study of the particular issue in education named in the question in each paragraph.
- Compare strengths and limitations in the same paragraph if possible.
- Refer to the research characteristics of the issue named in the question.
- Refer to research characteristics of **students**, **teachers** and **parents** and the context of studying in an educational institution such as a **school**.
- Try to apply these characteristics to the issue and method named in the question (not just to education in general).
- Use the item — it will contain hooks on the issue in the question and one or two strengths and limitations of the method.
- Refer to PET (practical, ethical and theoretical) issues for each strength and limitation.

> **Exam tip**
>
> If you refer to the positivist and interpretivist views of the method in the introduction, you have already begun to address one of the key aspects of an A-grade answer: a strong theoretical context.

> **Don'ts**
> - Don't refer to studies (unless it helps to illustrate a strength or limitation of using the method in relation to the issue).
> - Don't refer to why alternative methods would be better to study this topic.
> - **Don't write a conclusion — none is needed.**

Q05 can be broken down into different levels of response, discussed in the sections below.

Level 0 (L0): issue-only response

This response just discusses the issue raised in the question and on its own is unlikely to achieve more than a U grade.

Level 1 (L1): methods-only response

A major failing of students' responses to this question is answering it as a 'methods-only' question. Even if this type of answer presents an excellent coverage of the strengths and limitations of the method, it is unlikely to achieve more than a D grade.

In your introduction, remember to use WWWE on the method (see Template 2). If you mention why positivists or interpretivists use or do not use the method, you will be able to get the maximum possible marks for L1.

Level 2 (L2): application

Below are some general Level 2 application issues relating either to the research characteristics of studying groups involved in education (pupils, teachers and parents) or to the context of studying in an educational institution such as a school. You will be able to refer to some of these issues regardless of the topic raised in the question. In order to have good Level 2 application, these points should be applied to the issue raised in the question. Responses that have good Level 1 and have a range of developed Level 2 application can achieve up to a B grade, without even referring to the particular issue raised in the question.

To develop your AO2 marks, make sure you relate these points to PET and apply them specifically to the method referred to in the question. You should apply ethical issues relating to the context of studying schools to different methods. For example, in terms of the ethical issue of students missing out on curriculum time, it may be easier for a sociologist to persuade a head teacher to allow them to give out a brief questionnaire to students in a tutor period as opposed to withdrawing students for a lengthy unstructured interview during the time slot for a core subject like maths.

Pupils

Theoretical issues can be explained in terms of the problem of the researcher being seen as a 'teacher in disguise' by the pupil so that data may lack validity. For example, pupils may be reluctant to discuss their true feelings on teacher labelling or parental support in an interview as they may be afraid that this will get back to teachers or their parents. They may give socially desirable answers in an interview or questionnaire as they do not want to be put in a detention or be grounded.

Exam tip

Research characteristics refers to the main issues that a researcher would have to consider when choosing a method to study the topic of education. For example, due to pupils' shorter attention span, a sociologist should use a short questionnaire when carrying out research with pupils.

Exam tip

You should relate theoretical issues to practical concerns. For example, state that if students are rushing to complete a self-complete questionnaire or interview because the bell for lunch has just gone, their responses are likely to lack validity.

Exam tip

Be prepared to relate points specifically to the method. For questionnaires, for example, refer to pupils 'ticking any box', while for interviews you could refer to teachers not wanting to 'tell the truth' when certain questions are asked.

The language used in primary methods such as questionnaires and interviews will need to be kept simple and 'student friendly' in order to obtain valid data. For example, younger students may have problems understanding complex questions and sociological concepts such as cultural deprivation. For the Hawthorne effect and observations of lessons, students could either behave better than usual to get on their teacher's 'good side' or be more disruptive so they can get a teacher they dislike into 'trouble'.

Develop points by comparing how different students may prefer different types of methods. An interview may be easier than a self-complete questionnaire for a student with learning difficulties so that more valid data is obtained. Practical issues such as the questionnaires being too long may mean that pupils get bored or do not want to fill them in if they have to be completed out of lesson time.

In terms of ethical issues, pupils are a vulnerable group so as well as needing parental consent there is the issue of whether they are mature enough to give informed consent. Will Year 5 pupils really understand the purpose of the research even if it is explained to them? Sociologists will also need to be mindful of causing harm such as the potential negative impact on pupils' education. For example, pupils involved in an interview are likely to be missing out on lesson time at the very least.

Teachers

In a similar way, teachers may see the researcher as 'Ofsted in disguise' so this raises the theoretical problem that responses may lack validity. Teachers may be afraid of losing their job if they give honest answers in interviews or questionnaires on issues such as racism in schools. Again, with lesson observations, explain how the Hawthorne effect may come into play. Teachers who are knowingly sexist will not want to display their usual unfair treatment towards female students as they will be concerned that this will get back to their head teacher.

There are several practical issues that can be discussed in researching teachers such as timetable constraints and teachers being overworked and busy people. These factors may make it difficult for a researcher to arrange an interview or get a good response rate from a questionnaire. In terms of observations, teachers may be reluctant to allow the researcher access to their classroom and to take on the additional task of providing the researcher with a lesson plan.

Parents

Parents may see the researcher as just another teacher or even a 'social worker in disguise', again leading to theoretical issues. Their responses to questionnaires and interviews may lack validity because they don't want to be seen as a 'bad parent'. The biggest practical problem with researching parents is access, as they are not usually in school! A good research opportunity for sociologists is a parents' evening. However, as middle-class parents are more likely to attend, the sample may not be representative. Even if they attend, working-class parents who possess 'anti-school' attitudes may be reluctant to participate in an interview or open up if they see the researcher as middle class. In addition, parents from minority ethnic backgrounds may have language barriers which may affect the validity of responses.

Exam tip

Be prepared to discuss and evaluate strategies that a sociologist might employ to encourage a higher response rate, such as keeping the interviews or questionnaire short or paying for a supply teacher so that a teacher does not have to give up their own time for an interview. You should also evaluate such strategies in terms of whether they may reduce the validity of data or add to the cost of the research.

Exam tip

Remember to discuss strategies a sociologist might adopt to overcome the problem of access to parents (e.g. sending self-complete questionnaires via pupils), and to apply these to the context of studying education (e.g. the school's permission will still need to be obtained, certain parents are more likely to return the questionnaire and some pupils will not even take them home).

Schools

One of the main problems facing a sociologist when studying schools is the practical issue of access. Consent needs to be obtained from gatekeepers such as the head teacher or school governors for the research to go ahead. Even if this is achieved, head teachers may deny access to certain areas of the school or at certain times of the year such as during exams. Researchers may not be allowed to observe teachers perceived by head teachers as 'poor' as they may be concerned that this will reflect badly on the image of the school. However, once access is gained, sociologists have the major practical strength of a 'captive audience' and a ready-made sample stratified by year groups. Pupils are used to filling out questionnaires and they may feel they will get into trouble for not completing them, so a high response rate can be obtained. Group interviews can be arranged relatively easily but schools are busy places and there may be problems with finding classrooms to use for interviews.

In terms of documents and official statistics, there is a wide range of information available. Schools must provide certain information by law, such as on attendance, and statistics such as exam results and documents like Ofsted reports are in the public domain and easily available via the internet. However, schools have a duty of care towards their pupils and access to documentation such as school reports may be denied. Theoretical problems of lack of validity can be applied to education statistics, such as schools manipulating truancy rates to boost their position in the 'education market'.

If the question is on a secondary method rather than a primary one, do not panic! You can use some of the points that refer to primary methods and discuss how official statistics and some documents do *not* pose these problems. For example, sociologists using official statistics and public documents do not face the problems of access and gatekeepers, as they are secondary data and in the public domain.

Level 3 (L3): application

To achieve an A-grade response, the strengths and weaknesses of the method must be applied to the topic raised in the question and the item. For example, if the question is on using unstructured interviews to study the topic of material deprivation and achievement, the following response would be at L3:

> **Parents may give socially desirable responses which lack validity in the interview as they want to be seen as a supportive parent. For example, working-class parents may not want to tell a researcher that they can't afford to buy their son or daughter a sociology revision guide because they are on the minimum wage.**

It is much better to have two or three L3 points developed than to just list six or seven. You only need to use L3s well *twice* to get maximum marks. Two well-developed L3 points are enough as long as you have a sound knowledge of the method and a range of good L2s that are applied to the issue in the question.

Remember that you do not need to mention studies for the Methods in context question. If you do use them, it should be to illustrate a strength or weakness of the method in relation to the context of studying education or the topic.

Note that if the question refers to a specific group such as parents, you can still refer to other groups that sociologists may wish to study. For example, if the question refers to student subcultures, you should still discuss that researchers may wish to obtain the views of teachers and parents on this topic.

Exam tip

Remember to relate practical strengths such as having a 'captive audience' to theoretical strengths such as this leading to a potentially representative sample.

Exam tip

Try to develop the issue of access to schools to other practical issues such as the need for a DBS check which adds time and cost to the research.

Exam tip

Be prepared to apply contemporary issues to potential problems of using different methods. For example, despite exam results being generally regarded as 'hard' official statistics, schools have been found guilty of malpractice in relation to exam entries and manipulating data in order to improve their position in league tables.

Question 06

Outline and explain two...

Here is an example:

Outline and explain two limitations of using laboratory experiments in sociological research (10 marks; see page 74).

Remember you only need two paragraphs. No introduction or conclusion is required.

The first paragraph for the question above could be set out as follows:

- First sentence — state what the first limitation is. For the question above the first sentence could be: 'The first limitation of lab experiments is that they lack ecological validity.'
- AO1: **Explain** — Outline what the first limitation is. For the question above this could be to explain the concept of ecological validity, give an example of what this is and categorise the problem in terms of PET (theoretical for this limitation).
- AO3: **Analyse** — Unpack this with some discussion of the limitation. For example, for the question above you could refer to issues relating to PET (why interpretivists would reject it) and develop this through comparative analysis with another method (how field experiments don't have this limitation as they are not carried out in a controlled environment and take place in a natural setting).
- AO2: **Apply** — Use studies to illustrate this limitation. For example, for the question above state how in Bandura's experiment children were not playing in a natural environment meaning that the findings may have lacked validity.

EVALUATION — This is *not* required as there are no specific marks for evaluation for this question.

The same structure should be used for paragraph 2, which should focus on a separate limitation (such as ethical issues — see page 74).

Expect to find the following type of wording in Question 06.

For a methods question:

- two ethical/practical/theoretical disadvantages of a method or type of data
- two ethical/practical/theoretical advantages of a method or type of data
- two practical/ethical/theoretical problems researchers may experience

For a theory question:

- two strengths of a particular theory (e.g. Marxist, functionalist, feminist)
- two weaknesses or limitations of a particular theory
- two strengths of a particular type of theory (e.g. conflict, structural, social action)
- two weaknesses or limitations of a particular type of theory

Other questions:

- two reasons why sociology can/can't be regarded as a science
- two reasons why sociologists can/can't be value free in their research
- two ways in which sociological perspectives have influenced social policy

Exam tip

Do *not* use words such as 'however' for this question. AO3 marks are only awarded for analysis. However, if evaluation is within an analytical framework it should be credited.

Test paper 1

Education

(01) Outline **two** ways in which the experience of schooling may reinforce female students' gender identities. (4 marks)

> Remember to use bullet points and give an extra point if you have time. You must refer to issues in school that specifically relate to the gender identity of females. Factors such as double standards and the male gaze must be applied to the experiences of females within school. Similarly, same-sex peer groups would need to be qualified in terms of issues such as girl peer groups policing a hyper-heterosexual feminine identity within school.

(02) Outline **three** ways in which school mirrors work. (6 marks)

> Remember to use bullet points and give an extra point if you have time. To gain full marks for each point you must show how each way applies to education and the world of work. For example, points such as alienation must be explained in terms of how this occurs in school (such as pupils experiencing a lack of control on what to study) and the workplace (such as workers lacking control over production). Similarly, references to students having to comply with school rules on uniform must be compared to workers having a dress code to adhere to.

(03) Read **Item A** below and answer the question that follows.

> ### Item A
>
> Some sociologists have pointed to the differences in values between social class groups. It has been argued that while working-class subculture is characterised by a 'live for today' attitude, those from a middle-class background are more likely to postpone rewards. The level of education experienced is also seen to be a key factor in influencing the type of values that people will adopt.

Applying material from **Item A**, analyse **two** effects of parental attitudes on the achievement of different social class groups. (10 marks)

> You should spend about 15 minutes on this question. Divide your time fairly equally between each effect and write a paragraph on each. You could structure each paragraph as suggested on page 48. There is no need to write a separate introduction or conclusion. You are only required to give two effects and these must be applied from material in the item.
>
> The first 'hook' in Item A is the reference to working-class people 'living for today' compared with middle-class people being more likely to 'postpone rewards'. This should lead to a discussion of Sugarman's concepts of immediate and deferred gratification. This **must** be applied to how this affects the achievement of different social class groups: for example, how working-class parents are more likely to encourage their children to leave school as soon as possible in order to work, thus lowering their achievement. This could be evaluated by reference to Keddie's view that cultural deprivation theories are victim-blaming, or to the argument that material rather than cultural factors explain why a working-class parent may have to encourage their child to leave school as soon as possible.

The second 'hook' in Item A is the reference to 'levels of education'. This should lead to a discussion of cultural deprivation theorists' views that parents' education levels could lead to different types of socialisation: for example, middle-class parenting styles encouraging learning activities through educational toys. This **must** be applied to how this affects the achievement of different social class groups: for example, that being socialised with these types of toys will give middle-class students a 'head start'. This again could be evaluated by reference to material deprivation (e.g. that some working-class parents can't afford to buy educational toys) or the interactionist view that internal factors like teacher labelling are more important than parents' education levels.

It is possible to apply two effects from the same hook in the item. For example, for this question the first hook could have been applied to analyse two different effects: how the working class may underachieve (because of the parental value of immediate gratification) and how the middle class tend to achieve higher (due to the parental value of deferred gratification).

(04) Read **Item B** below and answer the question that follows.

Item B

Successive governments have implemented a range of policies aimed at achieving equal opportunities for all pupils in education. Some sociologists have favoured educational policies such as Operation Head Start, which attempt to compensate for the deprivation experienced by some pupils at home. Other sociologists have campaigned for governments to introduce policies aimed at reducing gender differences in achievement and subject choice.

However, some sociologists have argued that the most effective way to improve standards for all students is for governments to introduce market forces into the education system through policies such as publishing exam league tables.

Applying material from **Item B** and your knowledge, evaluate the claim that the main aim of educational policies has been to reduce inequality between social groups. (30 marks)

You should spend about 45 minutes on this question. You could use Template 1 for item-based essays to structure your response. Always read the question very carefully — note that this one talks about reducing inequality. As Item B suggests, you should refer to policies that have attempted to reduce inequality between genders as well as between social class groups. Policies that have attempted to raise the achievement of children from minority ethnic groups should also be discussed.

You could start with the 1944 Education Act which introduced the tripartite system and compare this with the comprehensive system in its impact on reducing inequality between social class groups (and between the genders in terms of access to grammar schools). You should use the marketisation policies introduced under the 1988 Education Reform Act (ERA) to evaluate the claim of the essay title. This should involve a discussion of policies that have increased parental choice and competition between schools. These should be analysed and evaluated with reference to the cultural capital of parents (Gerwitz) and school selection policies (Bartlett). The potential impact of these policies on increasing inequality between social groups should be discussed. You could develop analysis with a discussion of their potential benefits in terms of reducing inequality, as referred to in the second paragraph of the item. Be sure to discuss how policies from the New Labour government of 1997 onwards have often been aimed at both marketisation and reducing inequality. You could also refer to how policies have led to the education system becoming more privatised and how this has affected inequality. As well as specific evaluation points on policies, you could include the debate between the New Right and socialist/Marxist views on their impact.

Methods in context

(05) Read **Item C** below and answer the question that follows.

Item C Investigating the impact of teacher labelling on achievement

Many sociologists are interested in the ways in which teacher–pupil interaction in the classroom can affect achievement. Negative teacher labelling has been found to have a negative impact on pupils' self-image and may lead to a self-fulfilling prophecy of failure. This type of labelling may also result in certain students being placed in lower sets. Research also suggests that pupils can respond to teacher labelling in a variety of ways such as developing both pro- and anti-school subcultures.

One way of studying the impact of teacher labelling on educational achievement is to use participant observation. The researcher may be able to see for themselves how teachers label and how different groups of students react to these labels. However, as well as ethical problems, particularly with covert observation, the researcher has the issue of what role they should adopt within the school while conducting their research.

Applying material from **Item C** and your knowledge of research methods, evaluate the strengths and limitations of using participant observation to investigate the impact of teacher labelling on educational achievement.

(20 marks)

You should spend about 30 minutes on this question. In your introduction you could use WWWE, as outlined in Template 2 (see page 50), to ensure you locate the method in a theoretical context. Make sure you use the general L2 points outlined on pages 51–53 — but apply them to using participant observation and the issue of teacher labelling. To gain L3 marks you must refer to labelling **and** its potential impact on achievement.

A good place to start would be access as this is one of the first practical issues a sociologist would have to consider when using participant observation. The second paragraph of the item gives you a strength and two limitations of participant observation, so make sure you use them. For example, if the research is conducted covertly in a school there are only limited roles that a sociologist could adopt (such as a volunteer). Try to apply these clearly to the topic of the impact of teacher labelling on achievement. You will get some ideas from the first paragraph (such as students being placed in lower sets), but not do just copy from the item.

Labelling by teachers could occur in relation to gender, class and ethnic achievement, so use these to develop L3 points. For example, teachers will not want to appear to be racist or sexist in front of a researcher who they may see as 'Ofsted in disguise'. This relates to the Hawthorne effect and the theoretical issue of data lacking validity as a result. You could structure your answer around PET but be sure to apply the method to L2 and L3 issues in each paragraph.

Theory and methods

(06) Outline and explain **two** advantages of using unstructured interviews in sociological research.

(10 marks)

> You should spend about 15 minutes on this question. Divide your time fairly equally between each advantage and write a paragraph on each. You could structure each paragraph as suggested on page 54. You should only write about two advantages and there is no need to write a separate introduction or conclusion. Remember that these advantages should be related to unstructured and not structured interviews. You should categorise the advantages by using PET and analyse these using studies. For example, Dobash and Dobash could be applied to show the theoretical strength that as a result of gaining a good rapport with the interviewees they were able to gain valid data on a sensitive topic. Remember there are no marks for evaluation for this question.

Student A

(01) ■ Female peer groups will police each other in terms of how they behave. Girls who conform to the hyper-heterosexual feminine identity will give symbolic capital to girls who wear 'sexy' clothes and have a boyfriend.

■ Teachers may expect different things from girls than boys. For example, they may not expect girls to be good at PE as it is not 'feminine' and may tell boys in mixed PE lessons to not 'throw like a girl'.

> Two points on how schools may reinforce female gender identities have been explained with examples.
> **4/4 marks awarded**

(02) ■ Dress code. In school pupils often have to wear a uniform and some jobs require workers to wear certain types of clothing, e.g. business attire or a company logo.

■ Alienation. In school pupils have very little control over what they study. Similarly, most workers have little freedom and have to do what their boss tells them.

■ Rewards. While pupils get rewards from grades rather than enjoyment of the subject, workers get rewards from pay rather than job satisfaction.

> All three points have been explained with examples from education and the world of work.
> **6/6 marks awarded**

(03) As Item A states, it has been argued that working-class subculture is characterised by a 'live for today' attitude. This is a view supported by functionalists who argue that working-class students underachieve as a result of being culturally deprived. Sugarman argued that one aspect of working-class subculture was immediate gratification, i.e. that they would seek rewards now. Conversely, middle-class parents were more likely to socialise their children to defer gratification, i.e. to put off rewards to a later date. This can influence achievement between these class groups as working-class pupils would face less pressure from their parents to make sacrifices such as going out less in order to study hard for exams. Similarly, working-class parents would be more likely to encourage their children to leave school as soon as possible and work to get money as they would not see the value of education. On the other hand, Sugarman argues that middle-class parents were more likely to defer gratification and so would encourage their children to stay in education, postpone the rewards of a wage, and get more qualifications for their future career. However, this view has been criticised by Keddie for 'victim-blaming' and having a negative view of working-class culture. Also, Sugarman's study is very dated and it is likely that working-class subculture has changed since the 1970s and that most working-class parents today do value the importance of education. Also, some working-class parents may not encourage their children to go to university for financial reasons, not because they 'suffer' from immediate gratification and do not value education.

A second effect of parental attitudes on achievement relates to the 'level of education experienced' by parents. Douglas, another cultural deprivation theorist, argues that middle-class parents have higher aspirations for their children due to their own higher levels of education. They therefore take more interest in their child's education than working-class parents which would lead to them achieving higher. Due to the lower levels of education, working-class parents may not be as well-equipped as middle-class parents to support their children with schoolwork. Many cultural deprivation theorists argue that working-class homes lack books and educational toys, therefore children read less and have fewer activities to stimulate their development. As a result, working-class children are less prepared for starting school than middle-class children. Referring back to Douglas, he argues working-class parents are less likely to turn up to parents' evenings, which means they don't get to see if their child is having any problems at school. This may send a message to their children that their parents do not care, therefore they will give up and lose interest in school. However, Blackstone and Mortimer reject Douglas's ideas and argue that working-class parents may not attend parents' evenings because they may be working shifts in the evening or are put off by what they see as the middle-class atmosphere of the school. Therefore, it is not that they are culturally deprived and do not care about their child's education. Keddie would blame the middle-class bias in the education system for the relative failure of working-class children, not poor parental attitudes.

> Both paragraphs follow the structure suggested on page 48. The answer includes a clear reference to the item, appropriate studies and some good evaluation points. There is some good analysis with the comparison between working- and middle-class values concerning education, which is well applied to achievement.
> **10/10 marks awarded**

(04) As Item B states, the government have introduced various policies that attempted to reduce inequality between the social classes and males and females in education. For example, the aim of compensatory educational policies such as Operation Head Start in the USA in the 1960s has been to improve the educational achievement of working-class children in order to make up for their deprived backgrounds. However, more recently educational policies have been increasingly influenced by the philosophy of the New Right and have had the aim of making the education system more like a business, rather than reducing inequality.

> This is a good introduction which follows the AAA template (see page 49).

The 1944 Education Act was an early policy that was aimed at reducing class inequality in achievement. This was because it established free secondary education and gave all children in the country the opportunity to attend a grammar school by passing the 11+ exam. However, the tripartite system did not bring about equal opportunities in a number of ways. While functionalists would argue that the system was meritocratic, those from a conflict perspective would argue that the 11+ exam was culturally biased and favoured white, middle-class students. Marxists would argue that the policy reproduced and legitimated class inequality as it made it seem fair that middle-class students would end up in grammar schools and so achieve more than working-class students who largely ended up in secondary modern schools. Furthermore, it was not meritocratic in terms of gender as females had to achieve a higher score in the exam in order to get into a grammar school.

> This is a good account of the 1944 Education Act which has been applied to the question, evaluated and placed in a theoretical context.

As a result of these problems the tripartite system was largely replaced by the comprehensive system in the 1960s. The aim of this policy was to reduce inequality between social class groups by being non-selective. As there were no entry exams the policy was intended to give all children the opportunity to attend their local school and achieve. While functionalists would argue that this policy was successful in this respect as it was meritocratic and brought different social class groups together, Marxists would argue that it again reproduced class inequality as streaming in comprehensive schools meant that there was a tripartite system 'under one roof'. This meant that working-class students would still fail as they are more likely to be negatively labelled by middle-class teachers and put in lower sets. In addition, schools in middle-class areas tended to be higher performing schools so again this reproduced rather than reduced class inequalities in achievement. At this time, compensatory education policies were also introduced in the USA and the UK. The aim of these policies was to deal with the issues of cultural and material deprivation that were seen as a barrier to working-class pupils achieving. For example, in the USA Operation Head Start introduced nursery places and parenting classes for those from deprived backgrounds, while in the UK the government gave extra funding to schools in deprived areas (Educational Priority Areas) in order to raise the achievement of pupils.

> Again, this gives a good account of the rationale of compensatory education and the policy of the comprehensive system which have been well applied to the question.

Up until 1979 there was generally an agreement between different governments that educational policies should try to reduce inequalities between social groups. However, this postwar consensus ended with the Thatcher government which was influenced by the New Right view that 'market forces' should be introduced (as stated in the Item). As a result, policies since the 1988 Education Reform Act (ERA) have largely shifted towards marketisation rather than reducing inequality. This act introduced what David described as 'parentocracy'. This meant that parents had the right to choose which school to send their children to. In addition to league tables as mentioned in Item B, Ofsted reports were published which gave parents the opportunity to make an informed choice about which school to select for their children. In addition, the ERA introduced the policies of open enrolment and formula funding which meant that schools could recruit more pupils and receive greater funding as a result. Schools were also able to opt out of local authority control, be more selective and have more control over their budgets. All these marketisation policies have had the effect of increasing competition between schools, which the New Right argues is the most effective way of raising standards for students from all social groups.

> This gives a clear explanation of the 1988 Act. However, there is no evaluation of these marketisation policies in this paragraph.

However, Marxists would criticise these marketisation policies for increasing rather than reducing the gap in inequality between social class groups. Bartlett argues that schools that are higher in the league tables and are oversubscribed will be able to 'cream-skim' higher achieving, typically middle-class students, who are more likely to achieve as a result. At the same time, to maintain their league table position, these schools will be able to 'silt-shift' children seen as less able (working-class and SEN students) to schools that are lower in the league table and undersubscribed. If these schools can't attract students due to their lower position, they may have falling rolls and will receive less money under the policy of formula funding. As well as middle-class pupils benefitting from schools being more selective under marketisation policies, Gerwitz argues that, as middle-class parents have more cultural capital (such as knowledge about the appeals procedure and Ofsted reports), they are more likely to be 'privileged-skilled choosers', meaning their children are more likely to go to a higher achieving school. Conversely, Gerwitz found that working-class parents are more likely to be 'disconnected-local choosers' and so their children end up in a lower achieving school. As Ball argues, there is a myth of parentocracy, as many working-class parents have not got the same degree of choice as middle-class parents. For example, they may not be able to afford to move to the catchment area of a school high in the league tables. Therefore, inequality in achievement will be reproduced by marketisation policies that have enabled greater school and parental choice, as working-class children will be more likely to go to schools lower in the league tables, and so underachieve as a result.

> There is good coverage of the criticisms of marketisation policies relating to greater school and parental choice. It may have been a more effective strategy to include these criticisms while discussing these policies in the previous paragraph.

In addition to increasing the gap in inequality between social class groups, these marketisation policies could also increase the gap in achievement between males and females and different minority ethnic groups. In terms of gender, schools may see male students as less attractive than female as they generally achieve less well and are more likely to be excluded. Therefore, girls are more likely to be 'cream-skimmed' and so will achieve higher as they are more likely to be selected by a school higher up in the league tables. Similarly, certain ethnic groups may be seen as less attractive by schools and research suggests that school admissions policies can be racist. Due to language issues and a lack of cultural capital, certain minority ethnic group parents may lack the knowledge to be a 'privileged-skilled chooser'. For these reasons pupils from ethnic minority backgrounds may end up in schools lower in the league tables, meaning they are more likely to underachieve. However, a criticism of the impact of schools being able to 'cream-skim' students from particular social groups is that schools are only able to select 10% of their entry.

> There is some good application of parental choice and greater selection by schools to gender and ethnicity. The last two paragraphs have applied criticisms of marketisation policies to how these impact on the achievement of different social groups. However, they have not been applied to the specific claim raised in the essay title that the main aim of educational policies has been to reduce inequality between social groups.

As Item B states, there have been specific policies aimed at reducing inequality in gender achievement and subject choice. A range of equal opportunity policies have been introduced into schools with the aim of ensuring that boys and girls have the same opportunities. For example, the policy GIST encouraged girls to see science as a future career. This may not only have led to more girls choosing science and technology as an option at GCSE and A-level but could have also raised their achievement in these subjects. Due to the influence of feminist ideas, there has also been a policy to remove gender-stereotypical images from textbooks in schools. This may have helped to raise aspirations and therefore the achievement of girls. The policy of introducing coursework in the 1980s helped girls to achieve more as they are more organised. However, partly in response to boys underachieving there has recently been a policy of reducing coursework. This may explain why boys have narrowed the gap in achievement as they generally prefer exams as a method of assessment. Other policies that have attempted to raise the achievement of boys have been the 'Dads and Sons' policy that attempted to get fathers to be more involved in their sons' education and The National Literacy Strategy that focused on improving boys' reading skills.

This paragraph outlines a good range of policies relating to reducing gender inequality in achievement and subject choice which have been clearly presented with some good analysis.

While the majority of educational policies since the Thatcher government have focused on marketisation, the New Labour government of 1997 to 2010 introduced a range of policies that were aimed at reducing inequalities in class achievement. Sure Start was aimed at reducing social exclusion by providing support such as parenting classes and free nursery schooling for the disadvantaged. EMA and Aimhigher encouraged pupils from low-income families to stay on in sixth form and to aspire to go to university. However, some of New Labour's policies were more aimed at marketisation, such as specialist schools providing more choice for parents and the introduction of tuition fees. The New Labour 'City Academies' were an example of Blair's 'third way' as private sponsorship (a marketisation policy) was required to help improve struggling schools in deprived working-class areas (a policy aimed at reducing inequality). Since the Coalition government of 2010 the policy of academies has been pursued to encourage a free market in education rather than have a focus on reducing inequality. This government also introduced other marketisation policies such as Free Schools but did however introduce some policies aimed at reducing inequality, namely free school meals for all children up to year two and the Pupil Premium. On the whole, however, the main aim of educational policies of governments since 1988 has focused more on marketisation than reducing inequality, which goes against the claim of the essay title.

This paragraph has a good range of more recent policies and clearly applies these to the question.

Perhaps the main strength of the claim that the main aim of educational policies has been to reduce inequality between social groups is that, as functionalists argue, the education system is more meritocratic and in theory all students should have an equal opportunity for educational success. For example, the National Curriculum meant that all students in state schools should have the opportunity to study the same subjects and be assessed in the same way. However, especially since 1988, educational policies have increasingly been focused on marketisation and not reducing inequality. As Marxists suggest, some of these policies, such as 'parentocracy', may increase rather than reduce inequalities between social groups. Some educational policies may have different aims, such as introducing vocational education into the curriculum (e.g. BTECs), which was

This is a very good conclusion which follows the template suggested on page 49.

meant to provide young people with the skills needed for the economy. In addition, some policies may have more than one aim. For example, the main aim of the National Curriculum was to standardise how subjects were taught and assessed in schools across the country. This ensured that league tables would accurately reflect the performance of schools and give information for parents to exercise their choice of school. As well as assisting with the increased marketisation of education, this policy also helped reduce inequality between males and females as the National Curriculum meant that girls could no longer opt out of doing science for GSCE. This therefore narrowed gender differences in subject choice and achievement in this traditionally male subject. This illustrates how educational policies may have different aims and outcomes for pupils.

> Overall this response covers a wide range of policies that have aimed to reduce inequality between classes and genders in education and promote the marketisation of the education system. A policy that has a different aim (i.e. vocational education) is also mentioned. While the response does not cover any specific policies aimed at reducing equality between different ethnic groups, issues relating to parental choice, selection and ethnicity are discussed. Overall this response shows a very detailed knowledge of policies which are analysed and generally evaluated well and applied to the question. **30/30 marks awarded**

(05) Participant observation (PO) is when the researcher joins in the activities of the group studied. This can be either covert (where the researcher's identity is hidden) or overt (where the researcher's identity is known). Interpretivists favour this method as it provides findings that are rich in valid data. However, positivists would reject this method, arguing that it is unscientific as it lacks reliability.

> This is a good introduction following the WWWE template (see page 50).

First, in order to conduct the PO, the researcher must gain access into the school and will therefore need permission from the head teacher. They will also need to undergo a DBS check, leading to practical problems of increased time and money. If the researcher is overt the head teacher may be unwilling to allow the research to take place. It may damage the reputation of the school if it is found that teachers label students negatively on the basis of class, gender or ethnicity and that this negatively affects their achievement. The head teacher may also 'cherry pick' the teachers for the research so that the researcher is less likely to be allowed to observe teachers who are known to label students and treat them unfairly. On the other hand, as Item C states, if the researcher was covert they would have to find a suitable role. It would be highly unethical if the researcher took on the role of a teacher as this would not only involve deception but may impact on the education of students. A more appropriate role might be that of a volunteer, but this may not provide access to the areas of the school that the researcher would want to investigate.

> This paragraph makes some good attempts to discuss the characteristics of studying education. There is one brief L3 with the reference to head teachers not giving access to overt PO which is applied to labelling and achievement.

A major problem of overt PO is the Hawthorne effect. Teachers may see the researcher as 'Ofsted in disguise' and may be concerned about the findings damaging their reputation as a 'good teacher'. This may mean that they are less likely to negatively label students or give more positive attention towards students they favour, therefore meaning they achieve more. As a result, the findings would lack validity as they would not give a true picture of the way that they usually treat students. For example, they may usually label working-class, black boys as 'trouble' but if a stranger is in their classroom they may instead give them more positive attention. In a similar way students' behaviour may change if they see the researcher as a 'teacher in disguise'. They may not react to the teacher's negative labelling as they normally would do. For example, they may be afraid to engage behind the teacher's back in bad behaviour that negatively affects their achievement in case the researcher tells the teacher and they get a detention.

There are two examples of L3 in this paragraph in terms of how the Hawthorne effect could occur in overt PO for both teachers and students. This is clearly linked to labelling and achievement.

A practical problem for both overt and covert PO is that it takes time to see the impact of teacher labelling on achievement. While the researcher may observe negative labelling by the teacher in the classroom, they may not be able to measure the impact of this on pupils' achievement. The impact of labelling on achievement may well take place over a long period of time and it may not be practical in terms of both time and cost for a researcher to observe this process. Also, a researcher cannot be sure to what extent the student has internalised the labels given by the teacher. For example, a working-class student in an anti-school subculture may reject negative labelling by the teacher that they are 'thick' and may try to prove the teacher wrong and develop a pro-education culture by revising hard for exams at home. The researcher will not be able to observe this behaviour as it is outside of school.

This paragraph has some good practical limitations of PO that are developed into L3 points. The last point on PO not being able to ascertain whether students internalise labels does have reference to achievement in terms of revising hard for exams at home.

A theoretical strength of PO, especially covert PO, is that it provides the researcher with insight and validity as they see the interaction in the classroom for themselves. For example, they may observe how students respond to negative labelling in the classroom by refusing to do work set and so not achieving as a result. If the researcher is covert and takes on the role of classroom assistant, they may be able to gain the trust of the student. As a result, the student may open up and discuss how they feel about the teacher's negative or positive treatment based on their labels and how this has affected their achievement. For example, the researcher may overhear a student in a top set telling a friend how they are working hard because of the encouragement that they have been receiving from the teacher. During the observation the researcher may also be able to ask pupils questions relating to whether they feel that they are labelled and how this might affect their achievement (particularly if overt as the researcher will not be concerned about blowing their cover). However, it is unlikely that the researcher will be able to have in-depth conversations about these issues with students as it may disrupt the lesson and be overheard by the teacher.

In this paragraph theoretical strengths of PO are discussed and developed into L3 points. A characteristic of PO in a classroom is that it may provide the opportunity to ask students questions and this is applied to labelling and achievement.

An ethical issue with covert PO is that it involves a lack of informed consent as the students and teachers will not be aware that the person is investigating labelling and achievement. As well as deception, as the researcher is lying to both the teacher and students, the observation could potentially lead to harm. Students, particularly if they have special educational needs, are vulnerable and may disclose information to the researcher in confidence, such as safeguarding issues at home. However, the researcher will be in a moral dilemma as they may not wish to inform the teacher in case it blows their cover.

While there are some good L2 points here on ethical issues related to using covert PO in schools, these are not applied to the issue of labelling and achievement.

This answer covers a range of strengths and weaknesses of both covert and overt PO which, with the exception of the last paragraph, are generally applied well to the issue of labelling and achievement. There is good use of PET and the L3s cover potential issues related to studying both teachers and pupils. **20/20 marks awarded**

(06) One advantage of unstructured interviews (UI) is that you can get a rapport with the interviewee due to the informal nature of the interview. This practical issue leads to the theoretical advantage that interpretivists would want to achieve in that valid data can be gained. Unlike structured interviews, there are no set questions and the interview is more like an informal conversation. This means that the interview is more relaxed, and the interviewee feels like they are more in control. For example, the study by Dobash and Dobash on domestic violence was on a sensitive subject and it would have been difficult for the interviewee to open up. The fact that their UIs lasted for up to 12 hours demonstrates that a good rapport must have been gained with the women interviewed. The fact that the interview was informal and took place in a relaxed environment (in the women's refuge) meant that rapport was gained, and valid data was obtained. Similarly, as Oakley was a mother herself, she was able to get a good rapport with the women she studied during childbirth. Again, valid data was obtained using UIs due to the rapport gained by the researcher leading to the interviewee opening up about their experiences.

A second advantage of UIs is the theoretical strength that they can obtain valid data and uncover meanings behind people's actions. Unlike questionnaires, UIs don't have the issue of the imposition problem where the researcher decides on what questions and categories to use. As there are no set questions and it is more like an informal conversation, the interviewee can talk about issues that are important to them. For example, in Oakley's study, the women would all have had different experiences of childbirth and she would have been able to gain insight into their feelings about the effectiveness of antenatal care and so on. If she had only used set questions, Oakley may have missed out on factors that may have influenced their experience of childbirth. Similarly, Dobash and Dobash were

Both paragraphs are well structured and follow the structure suggested on page 54. Each reason has two studies which are used well to illustrate the two strengths of the method. It is a good idea to abbreviate words that will frequently be used in the answer as this will save time (see the first line of the response).
10/10 marks awarded

able to gain verstehen from the women studied as they were able to talk freely about their experiences of domestic violence and discuss issues that were important to them. As this is a very sensitive and personal issue, it would have been difficult for a researcher to predict what type of set questions were appropriate to ask.

> **Total score: 80/80. This response is likely to be awarded an A* grade.**

Student B

(01) ■ Verbal abuse, e.g. calling boys 'gay' if they do dance, reinforces hegemonic masculine identities.

■ The male gaze means that boys will view girls as sexual objects.

> The first point only scores 1 mark as the explanation relates to reinforcing male identities rather than female. The second point does not explain how the male gaze reinforces female identities. **2/4 marks awarded**

(02) ■ Hierarchy. While students are meant to accept the authority of teachers, workers have to follow orders from their boss.

■ You have to wear a uniform at school and work.

■ Fragmentation. School is divided up into different parts with lessons and breaks.

> The first point scores 2 marks as it has an appropriate explanation. The next two points are partial. The second point is not qualified and does not refer to dress codes in the workplace. The final point does not have an example that gives a comparison with the workplace (compare the answer of Student A). **4/6 marks awarded**

(03) Sugarman argues that the working-class subculture does not value education. Working-class parents are more likely to encourage their children to leave school as soon as they can hence they don't achieve well. They would feel that it would be better for their child to get a job rather than go on to university. As a result, they don't push or motivate them to do well in school. They are more likely to have the value of immediate gratification, which means they seek rewards now in the short term.

A second reason why the working class would underachieve is language codes. Bernstein found that the working class spoke using the 'restricted code'. This meant that they had limited vocabulary and spoke in short and grammatically simple sentences. As a result, working-class children would use this code in school as they had learnt no other way and would achieve less in English. On the other hand, middle-class pupils would achieve higher as they used the 'elaborated code' which uses a wider vocabulary and more complex sentences. However, not all subjects use language codes so it's not always important, for example in maths. Bernstein argues that working-class children fail because teachers don't teach them the elaborated code, not because they are culturally deprived.

> The first point is rewardable but it only implicitly refers to the item in the last sentence. It is a good strategy to quote the hook from the item. There is limited analysis and no evaluation. The second paragraph doesn't score as there is no reference to the hooks in the item. **5/10 marks awarded**

(04) Some sociologists favour educational policies such as 'Operation Head Start' as it helps compensate for deprivation experienced. However, some sociologists argue that policies should be more focused on bringing market forces into education.

Operation Head Start was introduced to deal with cultural deprivation that was felt to be experienced by working-class families. It wanted to give a head start to working-class students that middle-class students already had. This educational policy helped to improve their knowledge by making them go to kindergarten so that they were prepared for school just like middle-class students were. This would then contribute towards reducing inequality between working-class and middle-class students as the working class were given an extra boost that the middle class already had. However, other sociologists argue that marketisation policies helped to reduce inequality more.

Another educational policy that was introduced was the comprehensive system. This replaced the tripartite system and abolished the 11+ exam which was thought to be unfair to late developers who might start to achieve better after the age of 11. The aim of the comprehensive system was to bring working-class and middle-class pupils together so that it would reduce class inequality. A problem with the comprehensive system however was that it was up to the local authority whether they abolished the tripartite system, so it didn't cover the whole country.

Sure Start was another educational policy that helped to reduce class inequality. Like Operation Head Start it helped give working-class students a boost by giving them pre-school lessons which would help them achieve more equally to middle-class children whose parents could afford to send their children to nursery. This shows how the main aim of this policy was to reduce inequality between social class groups. Education Action Zones had a similar impact as the government gave extra resources to help working-class students who were materially deprived. As this would help them achieve better it would help reduce inequality between the classes. However, other sociologists would argue that marketisation policies such as league tables and parentocracy were more effective in reducing class inequality.

This introduction adds little and is largely recycled from the item. It does not set up the debate in terms of what is the main aim of educational policies.

There is a fair account of a policy which is applied to the question in terms of how the policy reduced inequality between social class groups. However, there is no specific evaluation of the policy. The last sentence is evaluation by juxtaposition only so does not score well. There is a missed opportunity to identify this as coming from the New Right perspective.

This is a very brief account of two policies and there is just one brief evaluation point. There is limited application to the question as it does not clearly explain how they reduced class inequality.

This is a basic account of Education Action Zones and Sure Start which have been partially applied to the question. While it does refer to how they may reduce inequality, it does not address the issue of whether this was the main aim of the policy. Again, the last sentence is evaluation by juxtaposition and does not connect this to the New Right perspective.

Parentocracy is a policy that was introduced to enable parents to choose the school that they wanted to send their children to. Parents became more powerful and schools had to try to attract them, as Item B suggests. However, this policy may not have reduced inequality between social groups. For example, middle-class parents would be better choosers than working-class parents as they had more cultural capital in terms of knowledge about how the selection process worked. They would be more likely to look at Ofsted reports and league tables and know how to appeal if they did not get their first choice of school. Conversely, working-class parents were either just not as interested in their child's education (as cultural deprivation theorists argue) or wouldn't have the skills to make a good choice. This is referred to as the myth of parentocracy and shows how some policies may actually increase inequality between social class groups rather than reduce them.

> There is some good analysis in terms of the differences between the social classes and parental choice. This is the best paragraph in terms of evaluation and application to the question.

> This response covers a reasonable range of policies which are applied to how they may reduce inequality between the social classes. However, it does not clearly address the issue raised in the question of whether this was the main aim of educational policies. While there are some attempts to evaluate, these are often by juxtaposition. There is also no reference to studies, sociological theory or which government introduced the policies discussed. While the last sentence is evaluative, the response lacks a conclusion to sum up the debate raised by the essay question. **20/30 marks awarded**

(05) To study this topic the researcher would need to gain access into the school. This may be hard because the sociologist may be seen as 'Ofsted in disguise'. If the sociologist is conducting overt participant observation (PO) where the researcher is honest about what they are studying, access may be harder. This is because teachers may be guilty of labelling students and the head teacher would not want the researcher to see this. However, if the researcher was covert they could lie and say that they wanted to be a volunteer rather than study labelling. This however leads to ethical problems as they have not got informed consent. As teacher labelling can have a negative effect on a student, the teacher may not want to be observed so they might also act as gatekeeper by refusing to allow the researchers into their class.

> There are a range of L2 points on access, but these are not well developed or applied to labelling and achievement. For example, the student could have discussed reasons why the head teacher would not want the researcher to see teachers labelling students (such as possible concern about the impact on the school's reputation). There are some reasonable L1 points on the method.

One practical strength of using PO to study the impact of labelling on achievement is that valid data can be obtained. The sociologist can get a first-hand insight into what goes on in the classroom. Being in the class will mean that they can see teachers labelling and how students respond to this. This is especially the case for covert PO as the Hawthorne effect can't happen meaning the data will be more valid. As the teacher will not know the reason why they are being observed, they will not change their behaviour.

> There is an error here in terms of categorising validity as a practical rather than theoretical issue. There are some reasonable L2 points, but these would need to be developed and refer to the impact on achievement to be rewarded as L3 points. The points on the Hawthorne effect only score as L1 as they are just on the method.

An ethical issue of using PO to investigate the issue of labelling is that the researcher will have to go undercover to conduct their study. This involves deception as the researcher will have to lie to those being studied. The sociologist will have to get a job in the school which will mean undergoing expensive training. They will have to risk blowing their cover which could end the research.

There are some reasonable points on ethical problems, but these do not score well as the student does not state that this refers specifically to covert PO.

One theoretical weakness of using PO to investigate teacher labelling is that those being studied may act up to please the researcher which is called the Hawthorne effect. Teachers may act differently and treat pupils more fairly than they would have done if not being observed. Similarly, the student may either act up to get the teacher in trouble or be on their best behaviour.

The points on the Hawthorne effect do not score well as the student does not state that these issues refer specifically to overt PO. There is an attempt to apply this weakness of the method to labelling but no reference to the impact on achievement.

As teacher labelling is a sensitive topic, it may be hard to get a true picture of labelling because teachers will not want to label a student negatively in case this gets back to their head teacher and damages their career. As labelling can be a self-fulfilling prophecy, it is not something that they would want to admit to someone they know is conducting research into the school.

This is a better attempt to apply the method to the topic as it refers to overt PO in the last line. However, to score as an L3 point the reference to self-fulfilling prophecy would need to be developed in terms of how this could impact on educational achievement.

This answer gives a limited range of strengths and weaknesses of PO and these are not always qualified as being overt or covert. While there are some L2 points, the attempts at L3 are not successful as there is no reference to the impact of labelling on achievement. **14/20 marks awarded**

(06) A major strength of unstructured interviews is that they have no ethical issues. As the researcher gains informed consent, the respondents are not being deceived in any way. They are also not going to be harmed and they have the right to withdraw at any time. However, when using a method such as covert participant observation, the research can cause real harm to those people studied. For example, Humphries deceived the men he observed and if their identity had been revealed then there could have been serious repercussions for them (e.g. their marriage could have been ruined).

While two appropriate points have been identified, there is limited development and studies have not been used to illustrate the advantages. There are some inaccuracies in the first point as unstructured interviews do have some ethical issues, such as potentially causing harm if the questions are too sensitive. The development with Humphries does not add to the response as it is focused on the disadvantages of an alternative method. **5/10 marks awarded**

Total score: 50/80. This response is likely to be awarded a high C grade.

A second advantage of unstructured interviews is that the interviewer will be able to explain questions to the interviewee. For example, an interviewee may find a question too difficult to understand because they have language issues. This can lead to more valid data as it will mean that the interviewee will be answering a question accurately.

Test paper 2

Education

(01) Outline **two** ways in which educational policies may increase inequality of educational achievement between social classes.

(4 marks)

> Remember to use bullet points and give an extra point if you have time. You must refer to policies that have increased rather than decreased inequality of achievement between social classes. These could include government marketisation policies such as 'parentocracy' and the introduction of league tables. However, school-based policies such as streaming, 'cream-skimming' or 'educational triage' could also be used. The removal of a policy designed to decrease inequality between the social classes, such EMA, would also score. To gain the additional mark you must refer to how the policy increases the likelihood of working-class students achieving less well than middle-class students.

(02) Outline **three** ways in which factors within schools may affect gender differences in achievement.

(6 marks)

> Remember to use bullet points and give an extra point if you have time. You must refer to factors within school and relate this to how they affect the achievement of males and/or females (see Question 1 on page 47 for more guidance on this question).

(03) Read **Item A** below and answer the question that follows.

> ### Item A
>
> According to functionalists, society is like a living organism made up of interrelated and interconnected parts. They argue that in order for these parts to work together effectively, there must be a value consensus in society. Additionally, functionalists argue that economies in modern societies are based on a complex, specialised division of labour.

Applying material from **Item A**, analyse **two** ways in which the education system might be functional for society.

(10 marks)

> You should spend about 15 minutes on this question. Divide your time fairly equally between each way and write a paragraph on each. You could structure each paragraph as suggested on page 48. There is no need to write a separate introduction or conclusion. You are only required to give two ways, and these must be applied from material in the item.
>
> The first 'hook' in Item A is the reference to the functionalist view of 'value consensus'. This should lead to a discussion of how the education system performs the socialisation function: for example, how Durkheim argued that shared values could be transmitted through the teaching of history or assemblies, or how education acts as a 'bridge' between the family and wider society (Parsons). This **must** be applied to how this is functional for society: for example,

how this process helps to create a sense of social solidarity in society and commitment to the wider social group. This could be evaluated by reference to Marxist arguments that, rather than transmitting shared values, education passes on ruling-class ideology that is not functional for society as a whole (Bowles and Gintis, Althusser). The feminist view that the 'hidden curriculum' passes on patriarchal values could also be used to evaluate the functionalist view that the socialisation function is positive for society.

The second 'hook' in Item A is the reference to the functionalist view of Durkheim that 'economies in modern society are based on a complex, specialised division of labour'. This should lead to a discussion of how the education system performs the economic function through skills provision. This **must** be applied to how this is functional for society: for example, how Durkheim argues that education passes on both general and specific skills that are positive for the individual and are required by employers. This could be evaluated by reference to the Marxist view that the real function of education is to produce docile, obedient workers for the benefit of capitalism, rather than to provide skills for the benefit of society as a whole. Evaluation could also be developed by reference to the New Right view that the education system fails to carry out the economic function and provide the skills required for industry.

(04) Read **Item B** below and answer the question that follows.

Item B

Research suggests that social class, gender and ethnicity can all significantly influence educational achievement. Some sociologists argue that differences in achievement are due to factors that take place in the home. For example, evidence suggests that family structure and levels of parental interest in education are crucial to a child's development. The linguistic skills that children have when they start school can vary significantly between different social groups.

However, other sociologists point to the importance of in-school factors as influences on achievement and how these may interact with factors outside of the school.

Applying material from **Item B** and your knowledge, evaluate the view that home factors are the main cause of differences in the educational achievement of different social groups.

(30 marks)

You should spend about 45 minutes on this question. Remember to use Template 1 for item-based essays. As Item B suggests, you should refer to class, gender and ethnic-based differences in achievement. As well as specific evaluation of home factors, you should use internal factors to evaluate the importance of factors at home for differences in achievement in the three types of social group. You should refer to a variety of different home factors, both material and cultural, as stated in the item, and clearly link the factors discussed to the achievement of the three types of group. You should consider the relative importance of different home factors and internal factors in relation to all group types, as well as the interplay between class, gender and ethnicity in affecting achievement. As the item suggests, you should refer to how external and internal factors may interact (for example, how teacher labelling may be influenced by language codes).

Methods in context

(05) Read **Item C** below and answer the question that follows.

> ## Item C Investigating the role of parental attitudes towards education
>
> Evidence suggests that there is a close correlation between parental involvement and pupils' achievement. Sociologists have identified a range of cultural and material factors such as attitudes to school, cultural capital, educational qualifications and differences in parents' income levels. In relation to both class and ethnic differences, the language spoken in the home and access to educational resources may affect pupils' achievement.
>
> One way of studying parental attitudes towards education is to use questionnaires. Questionnaires can be administered relatively easily using a large number of students, parents and teachers. As parents must supply information to schools by law, the researcher could gain a high response rate. However, some parents may be reluctant to complete the questionnaire, particularly if the questions are of a personal nature.

Applying material from **Item C** and your knowledge of research methods, evaluate the strengths and limitations of using questionnaires to investigate parental attitudes towards education.

(20 marks)

> You should spend about 30 minutes on this question. In your introduction you could use WWWE, as outlined in Template 2 (see page 50), to ensure you locate the method in a theoretical context. Make sure you use the general L2 points outlined on pages 51–53, but apply these to using questionnaires to investigate parental attitudes towards education.
>
> A good place to start would be with access into school as this is one of the first practical issues a sociologist would face when using a primary research method such as questionnaires. You could develop this point by stating that once permission has been gained from the head teacher, the researcher could email the questionnaire to respondents, so that they may not need to physically gain access into the school. This could lead to a discussion of different levels of response rate from teachers and pupils and parents from different social groups.
>
> The second paragraph of the item gives you some strengths and limitations of questionnaires, so make sure you use them as well as others you know. Try to apply these clearly to studying the issue of parental attitudes towards education. You will get some ideas on how to do this from the first paragraph, such as parents or pupils not wishing to tick boxes for questionnaires that suggest that they are culturally or materially deprived. Relate this to the theoretical issue of data lacking validity due to socially desirable responses. For example, parents may not want to admit in a questionnaire that they are materially deprived and don't have the money to buy their son or daughter a sociology revision guide. You could structure your answer around PET but make sure that you apply the method to L2 and L3 issues in each paragraph.

Theory and methods

(06) Outline and explain **two** limitations of using laboratory experiments in sociological research.

(10 marks)

> You should spend about 15 minutes on this question. Divide your time fairly equally between each limitation and write a paragraph on each. You could structure each paragraph as suggested on page 54. You should only write about two limitations and there is no need to write a separate introduction or conclusion. Remember that these limitations should be related to laboratory and not field experiments. You should categorise the limitations by use of PET and analyse these using studies. For example, use the experiments of Milgram and Bandura to show the ethical issues of deception and potential harm, or theoretical issues such as lack of ecological validity. Remember there are no marks for evaluation for this question.

Student A

(01) ■ League tables will increase inequality of educational achievement because the school publishes results therefore giving parents a choice over what school their child should go to. This means children from middle-class backgrounds are more likely to go to a 'good school' and are more likely to achieve as a result.

■ Material deprivation. Working-class children may be given less resources so won't achieve.

■ Cream-skimming and silt-shifting may increase inequality because middle-class students are more likely than working-class students to get picked by the better schools, therefore gaining a better education and achieving more.

> Two appropriate factors explained. The second point does not score as it is not a policy. This demonstrates that it may be a good strategy to include an additional point for small-mark questions. Sift-shifting has not been explained but could have been developed as a separate point to cream-skimming.
> **4/4 marks awarded**

(02) ■ Bedroom culture. As girls are more likely to engage in activities such as reading, they will develop better literacy skills and therefore achieve better in subjects like English.

■ Girls get more positive attention from teachers in lessons due to positive labelling. As they will have more attention from teachers, they are more likely to get help with their work.

■ GIST. This policy meant that girls would feel more confident in doing a subject like science and this could raise their achievement.

> The first point is well explained but this is an external factor so does not score. The second point scores 2 marks as the comment that teachers will 'help with their work' is enough to show the link to improving achievement. The third point also scores 2 marks.
> **4/6 marks awarded**

(03) One way in which the education system might be functional for society is that it socialises children from a young age into the shared values of society. As Item A states, there 'must be a consensus in society'. As the functionalist Durkheim argues, the teaching of shared values will help develop social solidarity. The ways in which the education system does this include the teaching of history and assemblies. These bind individuals together as they are socialised into the same values. As these values are shared within the education system, it ensures that school leavers are prepared to live in society and conform to its values, which results in education being functional for society. However, Marxists such as Althusser would argue that this socialisation function is not positive for all of society. He argues that as education is an ISA it transmits the values of the ruling class rather than values that are beneficial for society as a whole. In a similar way, feminists argue that the education system may not be functional as it passes on patriarchal values (such as encouraging girls to pick gender-stereotypical subjects like health and social care).

A second way that education is functional for society is in providing students with the economic function of skills provision. As Item A states, modern societies are 'based on a complex, specialised division of labour'. Durkheim argues that the education system prepares students for the economy by teaching general skills (such as punctuality) and specific skills (such as numeracy and ICT). This will increase their chances of getting a job after school. This shows how education can be functional for society as it gives students the right tools needed for the world of work. However, the New Right, while agreeing that education performs the socialisation function, would argue that it does not fulfil the economic function as too few school leavers have the skills needed by employers. Marxists would argue that rather than being functional for individuals and the economy, the real purpose of the economic function is to produce obedient workers for the benefit of capitalism.

> Both ways are explained in some detail and follow the structure suggested on page 48. Hooks from the item are applied to the question, and the evaluation in both paragraphs is particularly strong. Two criticisms are included for each point and these are located within a theoretical context.
> **10/10 marks awarded**

(04) As Item B states, levels of educational achievement vary depending on whether an individual is male or female or belongs to different social class or ethnic groups. Some sociologists such as functionalists would argue that external factors, such as cultural deprivation in terms of poor socialisation, are the main cause of underachievement in certain social groups. However, other sociologists such as interactionists argue that internal factors such as teacher labelling are more important.

> This is a good introduction which follows the AAA structure outlined in template 1 (see page 49).

In terms of working-class people and certain minority ethnic groups (MEGs), one external factor that can influence achievement is a lack of linguistic skills. Bernstein argued that there are two speech codes: restricted and elaborated. Working-class people typically possess the restricted code which has a simplistic form of speech, whereas the middle class possess the elaborated code which is used in schools by teachers and the examination system. As a result, middle-class students are likely to achieve higher. This external factor could be linked to the internal factor of labelling. Teachers may base their labelling on the language codes that pupils possess. For example, they may label a working-class student as 'deviant', as Becker suggests, because they use the restricted code. This could damage the pupil's self-esteem and lead to the self-fulfilling prophecy of failure as suggested by Rosenthal and Jacobsen. While a lack of linguistic skills is a form of cultural deprivation, Bernstein did not blame working-class parents but rather argued that the school system should be responsible for teaching the elaborated code to all children (particularly in subjects like English). Therefore Bernstein would reject the claim that home factors are the main cause of differential achievement between social class groups. However, it could be argued that, while language can be a key factor in achievement in English, it may not be so important in subjects such as maths.

> A good coverage of language which is linked well to internal factors. There is some good analysis of Bernstein which is well applied to the question. There is some brief evaluation but this could have been developed.

Language can also be used to explain why some MEGs underachieve. Bereiter and Engelmann argued that the language of low-income black students in the USA was inadequate and that this led to their underachievement. Similarly, those from ethnic groups whose first language is not English (EAL) may underachieve. However, research suggests that Asian students whose first language is not English will catch up by the age of 16. Additionally, the government has provided funding to all schools in the country to support EAL students. This will lessen the impact of the home factor of language on the achievement of certain MEGs.

> This is a brief account of how language may impact on the achievement of MEGs. However, it is well applied to the question and has some good evaluation with a specific criticism and use of a government policy.

Another way in which cultural deprivation may cause the underachievement of working-class and some MEG students is subcultural values and poor family structure. Sugarman argues that working-class subculture is characterised by fatalism (where you believe you have no control over your destiny) and immediate gratification (wanting rewards now). This will affect achievement as working-class parents may place less emphasis on the importance of education and may encourage their children to leave school as soon as possible, so that they underachieve. Conversely, middle-class parents are likely to socialise their children to defer gratification which

> This gives good coverage of the influence of class subculture which is well applied to the question via some good examples relating to achievement. There are also two good evaluation points.

means they will make sacrifices (such as revising hard) in order to gain benefits in the future (going to university to achieve more to get a well-paid job). However, it could be argued that working-class parents are being realistic rather than fatalistic as they can't afford for their children to stay on in education (particularly with the introduction of tuition fees). They may want their child to stay on in school but need them to earn money to help feed the family. Additionally, Sugarman's study (1970) is outdated and it could be argued that working-class parents in today's highly competitive economy are more likely to value education as important.

Some sociologists have applied the argument of subcultural values and poor socialisation to why some pupils from a black-Caribbean background may underachieve. Murray argues that black boys may lack a male role model as they are more likely to be in single-parent families. Similarly, Sewell argues that black boys may lack 'tough love' and as a result were socialised by 'street culture' and so could underachieve. Sewell recognises that internal factors, such as racist teacher labelling, caused some black boys to rebel and develop an anti-school subculture which would cause them to fail. However, he argues that external factors were more important in them developing an anti-school culture which would lead to them underachieving. Gillborn rejects this view (and the claim of the essay topic) and would argue that institutional racism within the education system is a more important reason than peer pressure from outside school in explaining why black boys underachieve. Conversely, Driver and Ballard suggest that the family structure of Asian people is more supportive and that this can explain why they have higher levels of achievement.

> There is a good attempt here to discuss the relative importance of internal and external factors with the reference to Sewell. The point on Asian family structure could have been developed.

Another external cause of underachievement for some social groups is material deprivation. Pupils who are working class or from some MEGs (such as the Bangladeshi community) are much more likely to be in poverty and therefore may not have the financial resources that can help achievement (such as being able to pay for a private tutor). Howard argues that these groups are more likely to experience poor housing which can lead to problems such as lacking a space to study, causing underachievement as students can't complete homework. However, it could be argued that schools offer after-school clubs and have libraries where students who are materially deprived could complete homework. Furthermore, these groups may have a poor diet due to lack of resources which can lead to illness or fatigue, making it harder to concentrate which could result in underachievement. However, cultural deprivation theorists would argue that poor diet is more to do with cultural choices as a healthy diet doesn't have to be expensive. As with cultural factors, material deprivation can

> This gives good coverage of how material factors may affect the achievement of working-class and MEG students. There is a good link made between internal and external factors and some good evaluation, such as the debate between cultural and material deprivation theorists.

influence what occurs inside school. For example, a working-class or Bangladeshi materially deprived student might be negatively labelled by teachers or face bullying from peers due to their parents not being able to afford a new school uniform. This may affect their achievement in terms of lowering their self-esteem or being absent from school.

External factors can also cause gender differences in achievement. Girls are often socialised into a bedroom culture and so are more likely to achieve as they develop better literacy skills than boys. While black boys may lack a male role model, black girls in single-parent families may have a positive role model as their mother may be providing for the family. This may encourage them to achieve in school as they value the importance of a good education for their future career. Driver argues that this is the main reason why black girls achieve higher than black boys. However, internal factors such as teachers labelling black boys as 'trouble', and therefore giving them more negative attention, may be a more important factor in explaining why black boys achieve less well.

> This has some good analysis on factors relating to gender but these lack breadth and depth. The evaluation with internal factors is by juxtaposition and there is no link made between internal and external factors.

Perhaps the main strength of the view that home factors are the main cause of differences in achievement between different social groups is that cultural deprivation theorists are correct to point to the importance of the influence of parents' attitude towards education. If working-class and black male students are not socialised to value education as important, then this is likely to affect how they achieve. However, perhaps a main weakness of the cultural deprivation theory is that, as Keddie suggests, working-class and MEG students are not culturally deprived but culturally different. She argues that these groups fail due to the education system being biased towards middle-class and white values. As interactionists would agree, Keddie argues that in-school factors, such as teacher labelling and an ethnocentric curriculum, are more important than home factors in explaining differential achievement. Additionally, as stated in Item B, external factors do not operate in isolation from internal factors. As research from Archer has demonstrated, the 'Nike identity' adopted by certain working-class, female and MEG students may come into conflict with the middle-class habitus of the education system and lead to underachievement. Furthermore, as Evans suggests, when looking at why certain social groups underachieve it is important to look at the interplay between class, gender and ethnicity. For example, statistics have shown that Chinese girls on free school meals achieve approximately 20% higher than white girls not on free school meals. This would suggest that cultural factors at home are more important than material factors in explaining why this particular ethnic group achieves well.

> This is a good conclusion which follows the template suggested on page 49.

> Overall this response covers a wide range of home factors that may cause differences in the educational achievement of different social groups. These are well explained, evaluated and applied to the question. However, there is less breadth on factors relating to gender, and evidence on MEGs could have included more range in terms of the different groups covered (the focus is mainly on black students). There is some good analysis and there are several attempts to link home factors with factors inside school.
> **28/30 marks awarded**

(05) A questionnaire is a list of standardised questions, usually closed, with pre-coded answers. Self-complete questionnaires are usually sent to respondents' homes and returned by post or email but can be distributed in person, for example in a classroom. Positivists would tend to use questionnaires as due to their standardised nature they are reliable and provide quantitative data. These data can be used to establish correlations and test a hypothesis. However, interpretivists would reject questionnaires as they do not give a true picture of respondents' meanings and so lack validity.

> This introduction follows WWWE (as outlined in Template 2; see p 50) well and shows good understanding of the method. There is a brief attempt at application, but this is not developed.

A major problem with researching this topic would be the practical problem of gaining access to distribute a questionnaire to students and teachers about the role of parents. Permission from gatekeepers such as the head teacher (to gain access to the school) would be needed. The school may be unwilling to let sociologists research a sensitive issue such as parents' attitudes, particularly if the findings from the questionnaire show the school in a bad light. For example, if the findings from the questionnaires revealed that teachers think parents lack interest in their child's education, the head teacher would be worried about the reputation of the school being damaged and therefore negatively influencing its league table position.

> There are some good L2 examples relating to access but these relate to studying education and have not been applied to the method.

Once inside school the researcher would need to find a way to distribute the questionnaire to pupils and teachers. Teachers usually are very busy during the school day and researchers would need to work around the teachers' timetables. They could give the questionnaire to them to complete in the staff room but are less likely to get it back if they do not wait around to collect it. With researching pupils, questionnaires have the practical strength of being easy to distribute in a school. For example, teachers could give out the questionnaire for pupils to fill out during tutor time. There would be a high response rate as pupils would be expected to complete them, and they might think that they would get a detention if they didn't do so. Another way of distributing the questionnaires would be via email. This would have the advantage of the researcher not needing to access the school, saving time and money as a DBS check would not be needed. However, unless an incentive was given it is unlikely that busy teachers or pupils (who would rather be outside playing etc.) would email them back. They may be seen as 'junk mail' or 'spam' and only certain people may return them, leading to a low response rate and potentially an unrepresentative sample.

> Again, there are some good L2 examples which relate to the research characteristics of teachers and pupils and studying education in general. While there is some application to the method, these do not score as L3 as they have not been applied to parental attitudes.

In terms of researching parents, consent would again need to be obtained. The school would not be able to give the addresses of the parents to the researcher due to the ethical issue of confidentiality. A way around this is to give the questionnaire to the student to pass on to the parent. However, this could lead to a low response rate and the theoretical issue of an unrepresentative sample. For example, a working-class pupil in an anti-school subculture may be less likely to give it to their parent to fill in. Additionally, parents from this type of background might have a negative attitude towards education so may not complete it. However, as parents are accustomed to giving information to the school (as the item suggests they sometimes have to do), they could just see it as another questionnaire they had to fill in from the school. One research opportunity would be to distribute the questionnaire to parents at a parents' evening. However, this may not be a representative sample as middle-class parents are more likely to attend, which leads to the theoretical problem of not being able to generalise from the findings. The wording of the questionnaire would need to be simple as students may struggle to understand sociological concepts such as cultural deprivation. This issue will also apply to some parents such as those whose first language is not English.

> This paragraph has some good L2 examples which relate to the research characteristics of parents and studying education. Again, they do not score as L3 as they have not been applied to parental attitudes.

A practical problem with questionnaires might be a lack of control for the researcher. If the researcher is not in the school, the intended respondent may not receive the questionnaire, or the wrong person may fill it in. The questions cannot be explained, which is another practical problem. The use of closed, pre-coded questions means that the findings are easy to analyse via computer programs so patterns and correlations (mentioned earlier) can be identified. However, the imposition problem may apply. This is where a researcher 'forces' the respondent to answer in a certain way as the researcher has already decided what questions are important and how people can respond. This undermines the validity as the respondent may not be able to express their true feelings with closed questions. Positivists favour questionnaires because they are objective, as there is no personal contact between the researcher and the respondent, while interpretivists reject questionnaires because a lack of contact leads to a lack of verstehen, as meanings cannot be clarified by the researcher. Another ethical problem is that the researcher needs to gain informed consent, ensure anonymity and not use questions that may lead to harm to the student.

> There is a range of good L1 points on the strengths and limitations of the method but these have not been applied to the issue. There are only a couple of brief attempts to apply these to education, and these are not developed enough for an L2.

Practical strengths of questionnaires are that they are quick and cheap. They could be distributed to a large, geographically dispersed sample. This could be useful as the sociologists could compare patterns and trends regarding parents' attitudes towards education in different schools across the country. This would appeal to a positivist researcher as the findings could be used to test a hypothesis concerning whether parents in working-class areas have a more negative attitude towards education than middle-class parents. Questions within the questionnaire could be about the income of the parent, as well as how supportive they think the school is, how they support their children's education and so on. This would enable the sociologist to make correlations from the quantitative data gained in terms of whether parents from a working-class background are less supportive and more culturally and materially deprived than middle-class parents. Similarly, the researcher could compare responses from different ethnic groups on this subject by having this as a category on the questionnaire.

> This paragraph has some good L1 points on the strengths of the method which are applied well to the issues of parental attitudes so score as L3 points.

A major theoretical problem with questionnaires is that they lack validity. Respondents may give socially desirable answers for various reasons. For example, the student might see the researcher as a 'teacher in disguise' so may not be willing to give valid answers in questionnaires. Again, a student in an anti-school subculture might see the researcher as a figure of authority and would not want to tick a box suggesting their parents aren't supportive as they may be afraid that their parent would get into trouble. Teachers might see the researcher as 'Ofsted in disguise', so again might give socially desirable responses that lack validity. For example, they may not tick a box stating that they don't communicate with parents in case this might damage their reputation as a 'good teacher'. They might worry that their responses could get back to the head teacher and that this could jeopardise their career. Similarly, parents may give socially desirable responses. For example, they may not want to admit in a questionnaire that they are materially deprived and don't have the money to buy their son or daughter textbooks. They would not want to be seen as a 'bad parent' if they are not very involved in helping their child. As a result socially desirable answers will be given, such as ticking a box which states that they spend two hours a night helping with homework when in fact they have to work a night shift in their job.

> This paragraph has some good L1 points on the weakness of the method which are applied well to the issues of parental attitudes so score as L3 points. While all points relate to socially desirable responses which lead to a lack of validity, separate L3 points are made as they are explained in terms of different issues for parents, pupils and teachers.

> This essay demonstrates a sound knowledge of the method. It is conceptually detailed, is put in a theoretical context and has a range of PET issues. There is also some good L2 application in paragraphs two to four which is well developed at times. The L3 points in the last two paragraphs have developed examples of application and as a result this response scores 20 out of 20. While a conclusion is a key component of 30-mark questions, it is not necessary in an answer for the Methods in context question.
> **20/20 marks awarded**

(06) One limitation of using lab experiments (LEs) is that they have many ethical problems. As they are generally covert and involve deception, LEs can lead to harm for those involved. For example, in Milgram's LE those involved were deceived into thinking that they had administered electric shocks to the 'learners'. This caused them psychological harm as they thought that they had inflicted pain and suffering. Some people involved even thought they had killed the 'learners'. This resulted in physical harm as three people involved had seizures as a result of the experience. In Bandura's Bobo doll LE, it could be argued that the children involved were also harmed as the researchers exposed them to violence and encouraged them to engage in aggressive behaviour. This could have caused long-term damage to the children involved.

A second limitation is the theoretical issue that LEs lack ecological validity. As they take place in an artificial environment, interpretivists would argue that LEs lack validity and verstehen. For example, in Bandura's experiment the children were not playing in a natural environment, so the findings may have lacked validity. The Hawthorne effect may occur as people may act differently because they know they are in an artificial and controlled environment. For example, the children in Bandura's LE may have seen the toys in the room, guessed that they were supposed to hit the Bobo doll, and done so to please the researcher. Even if the purpose of the LE is not revealed, as in Milgram's LE, the participants know that they are involved in an experiment so may not behave naturally.

The student has a good knowledge and understanding of two limitations. The problems are categorised in terms of PET and there is good application of studies to illustrate the disadvantages of laboratory experiments.
10/10 marks awarded

Total score: 76/80. This response is likely to be awarded an A* grade.

Student B

(01) ■ Middle-class parents have the knowledge and resources to research and choose the best schools based on the published league tables.

■ Working-class parents are less likely to be able to move to better areas to live in the catchment area of better schools.

Two appropriate policies are identified but these are not explained in terms of how they increase inequality of educational achievement between social classes.
2/4 marks awarded

(02) ■ Female role models. Schools are heavily populated by female teachers who can act as positive role models to encourage girls to make the right decisions in life.

■ Women in textbooks. By having more women prominent in textbooks in science, it gives girls the idea that science is a subject they should pick.

■ Coursework. The introduction of more coursework allows girls to achieve more as they are more organised than boys.

The first two points have appropriate factors but have not been explained in terms of improving the achievement of girls. The first point reference to 'make the right decisions in life' is not enough for achievement. The second point has been explained in relation to subject choice rather than achievement. The third point scores 2 marks.
4/6 marks awarded

(03) One way in which education can be functional for society is the idea that it creates shared values. Parsons felt that education acted as a bridge from the particularistic values of the home to the universalistic values of society. Therefore education is functional for society because it teaches students the values of society. This is called the socialisation function.

A second way that education is functional for society is the selection function. Those who achieve highest will get the most rewards, as argued by Davis and Moore. The education system is meritocratic and allows those who work hard and have ability to achieve good exam results and get a well-paid job. However, it could be argued that unemployed graduates have worked hard for no reward so therefore education isn't always positive for society.

> The first paragraph identifies a way in which education might be functional for society and this is applied from the item. However, it is not located in a theoretical context or developed in terms of analysis or evaluated. The second point is better in terms of development but does not score as a hook is not applied (the selection function is not mentioned in the item).
> **5/10 marks awarded**

(04) The main cause of differences in educational achievement is external factors outside of school. Some sociologists argue that material deprivation is one of the main reasons why there is a difference in achievement between social class groups. Material deprivation is when you don't have enough money to afford basic necessities. It is most common in working-class families, whereas middle-class families do have enough money for basics which leads to them achieving higher. Working-class families are more likely to have basic diets, meaning they are more likely to become ill and take time off school which then leads to them failing. However, sociologists argue that working-class students could catch up on work missed if they are absent.

> This is a fairly basic account of some material factors which has a common-sense evaluation point.

Another home factor which could cause differences in educational achievement between social classes is another material deprivation factor. Due to working-class people not having a high income, they may have a smaller house which means no place to study. This could lead to students failing as they can't complete homework. In contrast, middle-class families live in bigger homes enabling students to do work as they have a quiet place to study. In addition working-class parents may not be able to afford extra resources such as study guides and a private tutor. This could lead to working-class students being more likely to fail because they can't get the extra support they need. However, sociologists argue that working-class pupils could go to the library if they need a quiet place to study and there are revision resources available there that could help them achieve.

> This is a better paragraph on material factors in terms of both analysis and evaluation.

Another home factor which causes a class difference in achievement is cultural deprivation. It is argued that working-class families aren't likely to socialise their children into the values that are likely to help them achieve in school. Bernstein argued that working-class pupils speak in the restricted speech code which causes them to fail. As teachers and exam papers use the elaborated code, working-class students are less likely to understand and are at a disadvantage. In contrast, middle-class pupils speak the elaborated speech code which is favoured by the education system, therefore they are more likely to achieve. A criticism that Bernstein makes of the education system is that it should teach working-class students the elaborated code. Therefore he would disagree with the claim of the essay question as it is the school that causes underachievement (i.e. an internal factor) rather than the home.

> There is a good attempt to discuss and apply how language influences class and achievement using Bernstein. While there is no evaluation of Bernstein, there is some good analysis in terms of how language links to internal factors and this is applied to the question.

Another home factor is parental interest in the child's education. It is argued that middle-class parents are more interested in their child's education and will support them more in their learning, for example by buying them educational toys so they have a head start when they begin school. Douglas argues that middle-class parents are more likely to attend parents' evenings than working-class parents. He argues that working-class pupils will be less motivated to achieve as a result of thinking that their parents don't care about their education. However, it has been argued that working-class parents may not be able to attend for financial reasons and not because they don't care.

> This gives a fair account of Douglas which is applied to the question. The evaluation point could have been developed by reference to the debate between cultural and material deprivation theorists on why working-class parents may not attend parents' evenings.

However, it has been argued that internal factors are more important in causing working-class pupils to underachieve. Becker argues that teachers label working-class pupils as deviant and middle-class pupils as ideal. This labelling can lead to working-class students being put into lower sets and developing an anti-school culture which leads to them failing. An evaluation of this is that students can reject teacher labels.

> There is an attempt to introduce internal factors but these are not linked to external factors and so are not applied to the question. Evaluation is by juxtaposition only and the evaluation point on internal factors does not score as it is not applied to external factors.

> Overall the answer presents a fair range of external factors linked to the differential achievement of social classes. There is some reasonable evaluation of these and one attempt to link them with internal factors (Bernstein). Most factors are applied to how working-class pupils may be more likely to underachieve. However, there is no discussion of ethnic and gender differences in achievement. The answer also lacks any reference to the item and does not have an introduction or conclusion as outlined in Template 1 on page 49. There is not enough range and evaluation to get into the 19–24 mark band.
> **18/30 marks awarded**

(05) One of the main strengths of questionnaires is that it is easy to quantify the results, so they are easy to understand and compare. Quantitative data are data that can be counted and used to look for patterns and trends. However, questionnaires can also be qualitative, as questions can be open or closed. Closed questions have restricted yes/no answers or a box to tick, so you cannot elaborate your answers, while open questions can have longer detailed answers. Questionnaires tend to be favoured by positivists, who believe that sociology can be studied as a science, with quantitative data.

A strength of self-complete questionnaires is that there are no interviewer costs or interviewer bias. However, as the researcher is not there the questions cannot be explained. With questionnaires, closed questions might not present a true image of the parent's involvement. Parents might find some questions too personal and feel they are being judged, so might give false data, meaning the data would be invalid. Also, there may not be enough information within closed questionnaires to get a true representation of a parent's involvement. Also, as questionnaires are optional, a lot of parents may not answer it, or return it, and the response rate would not be high enough to get enough data.

A study by Hite illustrates that questionnaires may not be appropriate for studying certain topics in education. As the questions in her study related to sensitive and personal issues, there was a low response rate. This meant that, as only certain types of women may have responded, the findings could not be generalised. This meant that the sample was unrepresentative. She sent 100,000 questionnaires but only got 4,500 back.

A low response rate can be addressed by the use of an alternative method such as structured interviews. The advantages of structured interviews are that you can get a higher response rate as respondents find it harder to turn down a researcher if face to face, and it is more difficult for a respondent to lie face to face so potentially data are more valid. Interviewers can clarify questions, although they may have strict guidelines to follow.

The main advantage of questionnaires is reliable data. The main weakness might be a low response rate. If you triangulate methods and use structured interviews with questionnaires, you will get a better understanding of the role of parents.

This is a reasonable introduction, but it does not follow the WWWE template outlined on page 50, and as a result does not refer to interpretivist criticisms of the method. It would have been better to have a brief introduction following this WWWE template rather than discussing the types of questions that can be used in a questionnaire.

There is a brief L2 point in terms of the characteristic of parents being judged. This is linked to a problem of the method, but this is not developed or clearly related to the issue of parental attitudes towards education. The next two sentences are stated L1 points, the second of which is developed from the item (the use of the item should have been clearly stated).

While this develops the problem of low response rate mentioned in the previous paragraph, the study used does not refer to education so is of limited use.

The paragraph does not add to the response as it is focused on the strengths of an alternative method.

This conclusion adds nothing to the response. A strength and weakness have just been repeated and the last sentence on triangulation is a general point on methods.

This essay demonstrates some knowledge of the method. However, there is a lack of concepts, and strengths and limitations of the method are not categorised with PET. The main issue is that these strengths and weaknesses are not applied to studying education or the issues raised in the question. There is one L2 point but this is not developed.
11/20 marks awarded

(06) One disadvantage of using lab experiments in sociological research is that not all variables can be controlled which may affect the findings of the experiment. This means that the research is not reliable as not all variables are controlled. If the experiment was repeated it may not get the same results. It also means that the results gained from the experiment are not representative as another factor may have influenced the findings.

A second disadvantage is the practical issue that it may be difficult to find people to participate in the experiment. It may be expensive and take a lot of time. As lab experiments involve a lot of equipment this could also add to the cost.

The first paragraph identifies an appropriate limitation but this is not really developed, apart from the brief comment in the last sentence. There is also a misapplication of the concept of representative. The second paragraph has a weak and rather generalised point on the issue of finding participants. To improve, this would need to be developed in terms of why it would be difficult to find people to participate in a laboratory experiment. The student instead discusses a different practical issue which is not necessarily true of all laboratory experiments. In both paragraphs there is no application of studies to illustrate the limitations of using lab experiments. **4/10 marks awarded**

Total score: 44/80. This response is likely to be awarded a C grade.

■ Test paper 3

Education

(01) Outline **two** ways in which schools may act as a society in miniature. (4 marks)

> Remember to use bullet points and give an extra point if you have time. To gain full marks you must explain how each factor in school is reflected in wider society. Try to give an example to illustrate each point: for example, universalistic norms in society, such as equality before the law, being reflected by schools having universalistic norms, such as equality in the examination system.

(02) Outline **three** ways in which factors outside of school may affect ethnic differences in educational achievement. (6 marks)

> Remember to use bullet points and give an extra point if you have time. You must refer to factors outside of school and relate these to how they affect the achievement of a specific ethnic group (see page 47 for further guidance).

(03) Read **Item A** below and answer the question that follows.

Item A

> Since the 1988 Education Reform Act, a range of government policies have attempted to introduce market forces into the state education system. One aim of marketisation policies is to give more power to the consumer and provide them with more choice. In addition, policies such as open enrolment have given schools a greater degree of choice over their intake.

Applying material from **Item A,** analyse **two** effects of marketisation policies on increasing inequality of educational achievement between social class groups. (10 marks)

> You should spend about 15 minutes on this question. Divide your time fairly equally between each effect and write a paragraph on each. You could structure each paragraph as suggested on page 48. There is no need to write a separate introduction or conclusion. You are only required to give two effects and these must be applied from material in the item.
>
> The first 'hook' in Item A is the reference to giving 'more power to the consumer'. This should lead to a discussion of the policy of 'parentocracy' and how parents can use league tables and Ofsted reports to make an informed choice regarding the best school to send their children to. This **must** be applied to increasing inequality of educational achievement between different class groups: for example, that middle-class parents possess more cultural capital and so will be more likely to get their son or daughter into a 'good' school where they will be more likely to achieve higher (Gerwitz). This could be evaluated by debate between Ball and the 'myth of parentocracy' and the New Right argument that increasing parental choice will raise standards for all.
>
> The second 'hook' in Item A is the reference to the schools having 'a greater degree of choice over their intake'. This should lead to a discussion of how

marketisation policies such as open enrolment have given the opportunity for schools to be more selective and 'cream-skim' and 'silt-shift' (Bartlett). This **must** be applied to increasing inequality of educational achievement between different class groups: for example, that working-class students are more likely to be 'silt-shifted' by 'good' schools, which will mean they are less likely to achieve. This could be evaluated by reference to the New Right view that increased competition between schools will raise standards for working-class as well as middle-class students.

(04) Read **Item B** below and answer the question that follows.

Item B

Since the 1980s, in almost all subjects at GCSE level, females have outperformed males in terms of achievement. The impact of feminism, for example on equal opportunities policies in school and challenging stereotypes in the curriculum, has widely been acknowledged as a key factor in the improved achievement of girls. Such developments have also had an impact on subject choice. Other sociologists see factors external to the education system as being more important.

However, radical feminists argue that the experience of schooling reinforces traditional gender stereotypes and that this disadvantages girls in terms of both achievement and subject choice.

Applying material from **Item B** and your knowledge, evaluate the claim that gender differences in both achievement and subject choice are mainly the result of factors and processes within schools.

(30 marks)

You should spend about 45 minutes on this question. You could use Template 1 for item-based essays (see p 49) to structure your response. You should refer to a range of internal factors and discuss how some (such as GIST) may have affected gender differences in both achievement and subject choice. As well as specific evaluation of these internal factors, you should use external factors to evaluate the importance of factors and processes in school. To develop evaluation, consider the relative importance of different internal and external factors in relation to achievement and subject choice, and include the debate between liberal and radical feminists.

As Item B suggests, you should refer to the way in which schools can reinforce traditional gender identities and how this may affect both achievement and subject choice, for example through the influence of same-sex peer groups. The influence of external factors on how gender identities are constructed could be discussed to develop evaluation: for example, how the hyper-heterosexual feminine identity constructed by working-class girls (which may influence both achievement and subject choice) is formed outside of school.

Methods in context

(05) Read **Item C** below and answer the question that follows.

> ## Item C Investigating setting and streaming in schools
>
> Through processes in schools such labelling, streaming and setting, pupils may be polarised into either pro- or anti-school subcultures. This polarisation is more likely to have a greater impact if schools use streaming, as under this system schools group students together by ability for all subjects. Sociologists have examined how these processes are often based on class, gender and ethnicity. For example, anti-school subcultures, where pupils in the bottom set or stream may lack self-esteem and fail, are often dominated by working-class, male students from particular ethnic minority groups.
>
> One way of studying setting and streaming in schools is to use interviews. Unstructured interviews are effective in terms of gaining an in-depth understanding from respondents whereas structured interviews can be carried out relatively easily, usually involving a larger sample. However, for a variety of reasons, there may be questions in interviews that some pupils and teachers may not be willing to answer.

Applying material from **Item C** and your knowledge of research methods, evaluate the strengths and limitations of using interviews to investigate setting and streaming in schools.

(20 marks)

> You should spend about 30 minutes on this question. In your introduction you could use WWWE, as outlined in Template 2 (see p 50), to ensure you locate the method in a theoretical context. Make sure you use the general L2 points outlined on pages 51–53, but apply these to using interviews to investigate setting and streaming in schools.
>
> A good place to start would be with access into school as this is one of the first practical issues a sociologist would face when using a primary research method such as interviews. The second paragraph of the item gives you a strength and limitation of both types of interview, so make sure you use them. For example, some pupils (e.g. those with learning difficulties) may find questions difficult to understand, and teachers may give socially desirable answers (such as that they don't treat students in the bottom set or stream as 'thick'). Try to apply these clearly to the topic of setting and streaming. You can get ideas on how to do this from the first paragraph, such as students in lower sets being more likely to be part of an anti-school subculture.
>
> Also, setting and streaming by schools could be based on gender, class and ethnicity, so use this to develop L3 points. For example, students from an ethnic minority background may not want to tell the researcher (who they may see as a 'teacher in disguise') that teachers have put them in a bottom set because they are racist. This relates to social desirability and the theoretical issue of data lacking validity as a result. You could structure your answer around PET but make sure that you apply the method to L2 and L3 issues in each paragraph.

Theory and methods

(06) Outline and explain **two** theoretical problems with participant observation.

(10 marks)

> You should spend about 15 minutes on this question. Divide your time fairly equally between each problem and write one paragraph on each. You can refer to either overt or covert participant observation. You could structure each paragraph as suggested on page 54. You should only write about two limitations, and there is no need to write a separate introduction or conclusion. Make sure that you refer to theoretical problems such as reliability, representativeness, validity and objectivity, rather than practical or ethical issues. You should describe each problem in some detail and use studies to illustrate how the problems may occur in the research process.

Student A

(01)
- School acts as society in miniature as it is like a small community, e.g. in school and society you have to cooperate with people who are not part of your family.
- Pupils are streamed by their social class group.

> The first point gains 2 marks but the second lacks an example or explanation so only scores 1 mark. An appropriate explanation would have been that streaming reflects the class structure in wider society.
> **3/4 marks awarded**

(02)
- Research suggests that Asian families are more likely to have similar discipline procedures at home to those in schools. This means that their children will place a higher value on education so are more likely to achieve.
- Bereiter and Engelmann argue that low-income black American families are more likely to have language that lacks the 'correct' grammar. This meant they would not achieve well in school, e.g. in English.
- Some cultural deprivation theorists look at poor family structure.

> The first two points are explained well. The last point however only scores 1 mark as it does not refer to a specific ethnic group and hasn't been applied to achievement.
> **5/6 marks awarded**

(03) One effect of marketisation policies on increasing inequality of educational achievement between social classes has been to give parents more choice. As Item A states, the policy of 'parentocracy' (David) has 'given more power to the consumer'. Parents are now able to use league tables and Ofsted reports (additional marketisation policies) to make informed decisions about where to send their children. They will try to get their child into a school higher up on the league tables to get them a better education so they will achieve more. However, as Gerwitz argues, this may favour middle-class parents as they will tend to be privileged-skilled choosers and therefore have the cultural capital to interpret Ofsted reports and league tables. Conversely, working-class parents are more likely to be disconnected-local choosers so they will pick the closest school which may have a low league table position. The policy of parentocracy therefore favours middle-class parents who are not only better choosers, but more able financially to move to the catchment area of an achieving school. This will increase inequality between the classes as working-class pupils are more likely to underachieve if they go to a lower-achieving school. Ball refers to this as the myth of parentocracy as the policy creates the illusion that parents have free choice. However, the New Right would argue that this policy will increase competition in the education market as schools have to up their game to attract 'customers'. They would argue that this will therefore improve standards of education for all.

A second effect is that marketisation policies have enabled schools to select certain types of students. As Item A states, policies such as open enrolment have 'given schools a greater degree of choice over their intake'. Bartlett argues that schools high up in the league tables are now able to 'cream-skim' more able students as they now have more power to increase the number of students they take in (open enrolment) and be more selective (up to 10% of their intake can be selected based on an entry test). As schools may base their selection on class background rather than ability, this will mean that inequality between the social classes will increase. Whereas middle-class students are more likely to be cream-skimmed, working-class students are more likely to be 'silt-shifted' by 'good' schools to those schools lower in the league table. As a result they are less likely to achieve highly as these schools may have fewer resources (due to another marketisation policy of formula funding) and bigger class sizes. However, the New Right would argue that the increased competition between schools will raise standards for working-class as well as middle-class students. Additionally, as schools are only able to select a small minority of their intake, only a small number of working-class students are likely to not be able to get into a 'good' school and not achieve well as a result.

> Both paragraphs have followed the structure suggested on page 48. Both effects have been well analysed and evaluated, and material has been clearly applied to the question. While the focus has been on parentocracy and schools selecting, other marketisation policies have been applied appropriately. It is a good strategy for this 'apply' 10-mark question to quote the item and refer to the specific words used in the question, as this response has done.
> **10/10 marks awarded**

(04) As Item B states, sociologists have identified a range of factors that have taken place over the last 40 years in schools that have led to greater gender equality in achievement and subject choice. Liberal feminists would point to policies such as making textbooks less gender-stereotypical as an example of this. However, radical feminists would argue that gender equality has not yet been achieved in education and that schools are still based on patriarchy and reinforce a hegemonic masculinity. On the other hand, some sociologists argue that factors outside school are more important, such as gender socialisation in the home.

> This is a good introduction which follows the AAA template (see page 49). As well as AAA (use of Item and two opposing feminist views) this introduction also includes the internal versus external debate.

As Item B mentions, feminist ideas that boys and girls should have the same educational opportunities have had a significant impact on introducing policies into schools. For example, stereotypes in the curriculum were challenged and textbooks now have females in white coats in science labs. This will help girls see science as a subject that is open to all. Policies in school such as GIST have had a similar impact. If girls see science as a subject that they should be interested in (maybe for a future career), then this will not only raise their achievement but also make them more likely to pick science-based subjects as an option. In 1987, Kelly found that science was presented as a male subject, which put girls off choosing it at GCSE. However, science was made compulsory with the introduction of the National Curriculum in the following year. Kelly argues that this policy helped to reduce inequalities and meant girls would inevitably achieve better in science and be more likely to opt for it at A-level. However, it could be argued that external policies have had a greater impact on raising girls' achievement. For example, the Equal Pay Act could be a more important factor as it encouraged girls to pursue a career instead of settling for the housewife-mother role, and therefore to work hard in school. Radical feminists would reject the claim of liberal feminists that such internal policies have led to greater gender equality. They would argue that double standards, verbal abuse and the male gaze are all examples of how the school experience can reinforce gender inequality. For example, girls who pick PE may be labelled as 'butch' by their peers (Dewar 1990) which means they may not pick this subject as an option and so not achieve as highly as they could have done.

> This paragraph has a good discussion of how policies introduced in schools may have influenced gender achievement and subject choice. There is some good evaluation using external factors and criticisms from radical feminists.

Radical feminists would argue that there are other factors in school that could lead to gender-stereotypical subject choices. Students often choose subjects that lie within their gender domain. Boys may also be policed to conform to traditional gender identities by their peers and may not pick subjects such as dance out of fear of being labelled by their peers as 'gay'. They may also get gender-stereotypical advice from teachers who may reinforce the traditional view of masculinity. For example, they may be put off opting to do health and social care if a teacher advises that this would not help them with their future career. However, it could be argued that external factors such as parents buying gender-stereotypical toys are a more importance influence on subject choice.

> Internal factors relating to subject choice are discussed further and located within a theoretical context. There is a good evaluation point on external factors, but this could have been developed.

Another internal factor affecting the gender achievement gap has been the introduction of coursework. Gorard found that the achievement gap in gender increased sharply in favour of girls from 1989 when coursework was introduced. It has been argued that girls are better at coursework because they are more organised (Mitsos and Browne 1998). They are also more likely to pick subjects that are based on coursework as a result. Boys therefore achieved less than girls because this assessment method favours girls. However, it could be argued that this difference in achievement is influenced by external factors. For example, girls might be more organised because of the way they are socialised at home. Additionally, research suggests that girls have a 'bedroom culture' that means they have better literacy skills than boys. This external factor may contribute to why girls do better at coursework and generally achieve higher than boys. This argument is also out of date as over the last few years there has been less coursework in assessments. However, the fact that boys are starting to narrow the gender achievement gap could be due to the fact that assessments are now mainly based on exams, illustrating that the way students are assessed could be a key factor influencing gender and achievement.

> There is a good discussion of the impact of coursework on achievement which is also linked briefly to subject choice. There are some very good analysis and evaluation on the impact of coursework which is related to the influence of external factors on both achievement and subject choice.

Role models have also been identified as a key factor in influencing gender differences in achievement. As the majority of teachers (particularly in primary schools) are female, girls have a positive role model to aspire to. For example, it has been found that only about 20% of primary school teachers are male, meaning that at an age where gender socialisation occurs, education is presented as 'feminine'. As girls are given positive role models, they may work harder in school to gain the qualifications needed for a well-paid job. This results in the 'feminisation' of education where boys see education as 'girly' so are not motivated to achieve. However, Francis found that about two thirds of primary school boys aged 7 to 8 did not consider the gender of the teacher to be important. This suggests that the internal factor of a lack of a male role model in school does not affect the achievement of boys. The importance of role models could however be an external factor. For example, the rise in divorce and lone-parent families has provided the positive role model for girls of the financially independent mother. As a result this may motivate them to achieve and pick non-stereotypical subjects in order to get qualifications for the career they want to follow, such as IT. Similarly, boys may see education as feminine because they were read to by their mother, rather than from the influence of internal factors such as a lack of male teachers.

> There is some good analysis of the potential impact of both internal and external role models on achievement and subject choice. There is some good evaluation and points are applied well to the question.

Peer groups within school also reinforce traditional gender identities and can lead to gender inequality in both subject choice and achievement. This may be influenced by social class and ethnicity as well as by gender. Mac an Ghaill found that different masculine identities in school were reinforced by different social class groups. He found that the majority of working-class boys saw achievement as being in the female domain. These 'macho lads' were dismissive of boys who wanted to achieve, labelling them as 'dickhead achievers'. This was a way of policing their identity and reinforcing the traditional working-class masculine identity of not valuing education. Conversely, it was found that middle-class boys wanted to achieve without appearing to try. Female peer groups also reinforce traditional gender identities that may affect achievement and subject choice. Archer (2010) found that working-class girls have a hyper-heterosexual feminine identity which values 'being loud' and having a boyfriend to gain symbolic capital (status) from peers over working hard to achieve. On the other hand, middle-class girls are more likely to perform the 'boffin identify' which values achievement. The need to conform to these identities can also influence subject choice: for example, middle-class girls with the boffin identity may be policed by their peers to not pick a non-academic subject like textiles. However, the influence of gender identities can be caused by external as well as internal factors. The 'Nike identity', for example, may be part of the working-class gender identity for both males and females. This originates from outside the school but will conflict with the school's middle-class habitus, which may cause symbolic violence leading to underachievement.

> This gives some very sophisticated analysis of the impact of gender identity and social class on gender achievement and subject choice. There is good application of studies and a discussion of the internal versus external debate.

Perhaps the main strength of the claim that internal factors are the main cause of gender difference in achievement and subject choice is that policies such as GIST and the National Curriculum have clearly made a difference in terms of which subjects boys and girls choose and have also given them an equal opportunity to achieve. Perhaps the main weakness of this claim is that it ignores the influence of external factors. Clearly both internal and external factors contribute to gender differences in achievement and subject choice, and, as has been demonstrated, they may interact with each other.

> While it has a good concluding point about the main strength of the question's claim, this conclusion does not fully follow the template suggested on page 49. The sentence about the main weakness and the last sentence make good points, but they are not developed with examples. It would have been useful to return to the debate between liberal and radical feminists that was referred to earlier in the response.

> Overall this response covers a wide range of internal factors that may cause gender differences in achievement and subject choice. These are well explained and applied to the question. The response is conceptually detailed and has a good range of studies that are applied well to the question. There is some sophisticated analysis and several attempts to discuss the relative importance of internal and external factors. While evaluation is very strong, occasionally points could have been developed, particularly in the conclusion.
> **30/30 marks awarded**

(05) An unstructured interview (UI) is an informal conversation between the researcher and respondent which has no set format. Interpretivists favour UIs as they allow the respondent to take control of the interview leading to valid data. Structured interviews (SIs), on the other hand, have set questions and as a result are favoured by positivists due to their reliability. Interpretivists would however argue that SIs lack validity due to the imposition theory as the researcher has already decided the questions and the categories.

> This is a good introduction following the WWWE template (see page 50).

The researcher will need to gain access into the school through the governors or head teacher. Once they have done so, they will need to contact the teacher to gain access to the students. However, the head teacher may refuse the researcher access if they know that their streaming system is biased against students from a working-class or minority ethnic group (MEG) background. The head teacher would be concerned that the findings of the research would show the school in a bad light and so have a negative impact on the league table position of the school. Access would also involve being subject to a DBS check which costs time and money. Access may also be limited by timetabling issues. Researchers will have to liaise with head teachers and teachers over which lessons to withdraw students from. For example, teachers may not want students to miss certain lessons such as revision sessions for core subjects.

> There is a range of good L2 points. However, only one of these is developed into a strong L2 point as it refers to the characteristic of a school being concerned about its reputation if it streamed unfairly. As points are not specifically applied to the method, there is no L3.

This could also lead to an unrepresentative sample as teachers may prevent lower-stream students from being interviewed as the streaming could have a negative impact on their achievement. They may also only allow higher-streamed students to be interviewed because missing a lesson may not affect their achievement as much. Pupils may also refuse to be interviewed, especially if they are in an anti-school subculture, which is more likely with students in a lower stream. Conversely students in a pro-school culture in the top sets and streams may be more willing to be involved.

> Again there are some good L2 points (referring to characteristics of teachers and pupils) but these are not specifically applied to the method.

A strength of using UIs is that a rapport can be built between the researcher and the respondent because of the informal nature of the interview. Interpretivists would argue that this leads to the theoretical strength of the data being more valid. It would be beneficial to use a younger interviewer because they may be more likely than an older researcher to be able to build a rapport with students as students are less likely to see them as a 'teacher in disguise'. The students will therefore feel more comfortable in discussing how streaming has affected them (e.g. that they have lost confidence as they are in a bottom stream or that the teachers underestimate their ability).

In contrast, a failing student in a pro-school subculture in a top stream may be less likely to open up because they don't want the researcher to tell the teacher that they have given up on their studies. Furthermore, a young, working-class interviewer could gain more verstehen with a working-class student in a lower stream. They could communicate more on their level and be aware of 'urban slang'. Similarly, a MEG student from a lower stream may be more likely to discuss their feeling that streaming is racist in their school if the researcher is from a MEG background.

A practical strength of UIs is that they are very flexible. However, they have the theoretical weakness that it may be easier for a respondent to lie. Teachers may lie about the fact that they make decisions about streaming students on the basis of class, gender or ethnicity. They might give socially desirable responses to questions and not want to be seen as a bad teacher by the researcher, who they might see as 'Ofsted in disguise'. They may be afraid that, if they were honest about how they stream students, this would get back to the head teacher and they might be in danger of losing their job. Alternatively, the teacher may select students in a high stream to be interviewed (for either SIs or UIs) so they get good feedback. These students are more likely to be pro-school and share the educational values of the school. They too might give socially desirable answers in the interview about the streaming system in their school, such as saying it is meritocratic. They might be concerned that any negative comments they do make about streaming may get back to the teacher and mean that they are moved down a stream as a result. As the interviewer may be seen as a 'teacher in disguise', they may give socially desirable answers leading to the theoretical issue that the data will lack validity.

The researcher will need to gain parental permission because both types of interviews involve direct contact with the pupils. This leads to the practical problem that it can be time-consuming and may have a low response rate. A researcher could send permission slips home with students which could be a cheap way to do this. However, pupils in a lower stream might be less likely to give the slip to their parents, for example because they don't want them to know about them being in a lower stream and that they are underachieving. Alternatively, some MEG parents may not have English as their first language or may not understand what streaming is so may not give permission for their child to take part. The sample may therefore be unrepresentative if only certain types of parents return the

This paragraph has a good L3 point on how the rapport gained (a strength of the method) may lead to gaining valid data from identified pupils. There is a good discussion of the theoretical strength of UIs which is well applied to the characteristics of different types of students and streaming.

Again this paragraph has a range of good L3 points. There is a good discussion of the theoretical weakness of socially desirable responses (for both types of interview) which is well applied to the characteristics of both teachers and pupils in relation to streaming.

reply slip and give permission. The topic of setting and streaming can also raise ethical issues as it could cause harm to the interviewee. This is particularly the case for an SI as the interviewer is 'in control' of the interview. For example, a vulnerable student with social and emotional needs might feel pressured to respond to a question relating to how their teachers treat students in lower streams as 'thick'. As a UI is more like a chat, the student might not feel as pressured to respond. They are more likely to feel that they have the 'right to withdraw' and may not feel they have to give an answer.

A strength of SIs, as Item C states, is that they are quicker than UIs and so have the practical advantage of being able to have a larger sample. This will mean that the sample is more representative and the researcher can generalise from the findings. However, a weakness is that SIs do not allow for verstehen as the researcher is in control of the interview and sets the agenda in terms of the questions being asked and the responses that can be given. For example, if a student has learning difficulties they may not understand the questions.

> This has good L3 points on the research characteristics of pupils in relation to a practical issue (response rate) and ethical issues of the method which are well applied to the characteristics of pupils in lower streams. There are some other good L2 points but these are not applied to streaming.

> While there are some good L1 points here on SIs, these have not been applied to the issue. There is a brief application point made in terms of studying education in the last sentence but this is not developed.

This answer covers a range of strengths and weaknesses of both types of interviews. There are attempts to apply these to the issue of setting and streaming in paragraphs four to six. There is good use of PET and the L3s cover potential issues relating to studying both teachers and pupils. While the response focuses more on UIs, there is enough application to gain a maximum mark.
20/20 marks awarded

(06) Perhaps the biggest theoretical problem with both overt and covert participant observation (CPO) is its lack of reliability. Positivists would argue that participant observation (PO) is impossible to replicate as it isn't standardised. They would argue that as a result the method is unscientific as the original study cannot be replicated to see if the findings are true. While CPO studies such as Patrick's research on a Glasgow gang lead to valid data, it would be impossible for another researcher to repeat what Patrick did and get the same results. Although Patrick was a teacher he was young enough to be able to fit in with the gang. Also, he had access to the gang through his contact with the gang leader Tim. It would be extremely difficult for another researcher to gain access to the gang in the same way to repeat the study to test if the findings were accurate. An additional problem is that the dynamics of the group would have been changed if a different researcher attempted to study the same gang.

> In the first paragraph there is good coverage of the issue of lack of reliability which is linked to the positivist perspective and explained with the use of a study.

Despite it being useful to understand the meanings of social groups through the researcher taking part in their activities as interpretivists argue, a second theoretical problem with PO is that it may lack validity. This is particularly an issue for overt participant observation (OPO) due to the Hawthorne effect. As the group being studied know that they are being observed, they may change their behaviour during the activities that the researcher is taking part in. In Punch's study of police in Amsterdam, the officers he spent time with might not have behaved normally. For example, they might not have shown him how they usually treated people during stop and search activities if they were afraid of getting reported for being too aggressive to the public. Similarly, the senior Moonies in Barker's study involving OPO may not have shown her how they 'brainwashed' new members to stay in the group. In both studies the data may not have been a valid picture of the group's normal behaviour. While CPO doesn't have the problem of the Hawthorne effect, which is why interpretivists prefer it to OPO, the fact that the researcher becomes a new member of the group may cause suspicion and change the dynamic of the group, again raising validity problems.

In the second paragraph studies are again used well to illustrate the issue of the Hawthorne effect and a lack of validity. There is some good analysis with the comparison between overt and covert participant observation concerning lack of validity.
10/10 marks awarded

Total score: 78/80. This answer is likely to be awarded an A* grade.

Knowledge check answers

1 Possible answers include: providing specific skills such as IT; providing general skills such as team work; bridging the gap between the family and the workplace; socialising pupils into values required in the economy such as punctuality; role allocation.

2 Possible answers include: knowledge of the arts such as Shakespeare and classical music; experiences such as visits to museums and art galleries; more expressive language; being socialised into manners that do not question authority; parents having a better knowledge of the education system and admissions procedures.

3 Possible answers include: creating a two-tier education system; the myth of parentocracy, as greater selection disadvantages males, working-class pupils and certain ethnic minority groups; middle-class parents having more cultural capital so that they are 'more skilled choosers' of schools; Marxist criticisms that it reproduces inequality.

4 Possible answers include: there is still a National Curriculum that the majority of students follow; the majority of students follow the same types of assessment such as GCSE; there is a limited amount of vocational education; there is a lack of general preparation for the diverse needs of the economy, for example business leaders have called for more 'soft' life skills to be taught in schools.

5 Possible answers include: poor diet and health; poor housing; lack of educational resources such as textbooks and calculators; unable to afford private tuition; unable to afford the costs of higher education; unable to afford to live in an area of a higher-achieving school.

6 Cultural deprivation theory argues that working-class people lack the values needed for success in education whereas cultural capital argues that middle-class people possess the values which enable them to achieve.

7 Possible answers include: pupils can reject teacher labels; functionalists argue that subcultural values develop from the poor values that working-class students may bring into school; neo-Marxist Willis argues that subcultures develop as a result of working-class students rejecting the values of the school; teacher labelling can also result in students developing pro-school cultures.

8 Possible answers, based on the work of cultural deprivation theorists, include:
- *Black-Caribbean students*: language dialect; lack of a male role model (for boys: Murray, 1984; family structure being less resistant to racism: Pryce, 1979).
- *Asian students*: having English as a second language; the 'controlling' nature of family structure (particularly for girls: Khan, 1979).
- *Eastern European and other immigrant groups*: having English as a second language.

For all groups you could refer to a lack of cultural capital, for example in relation to parental choice.

9 Possible answers include: the ethnocentric curriculum; schools giving a low priority to race-related issues such as dealing with racist incidents; ethnic minority groups being placed into lower sets due to issues such as language differences; Asian pupils, particularly girls, getting less attention from teachers; cultural traditions being ignored.

10 Possible answers include: toys bought by parents; games and activities parents and teachers encourage; gendered subject images; gender-stereotypical peer pressure; sex-typing of occupations.

11 Possible answers include: schools being allowed to opt out of local authority control and become academies; businesses and other groups being allowed to set up free schools; business sponsorship of schools; allowing educational services to be delivered by the private sector; formula funding; the PPPs initiative where private companies built state schools.

12 Possible answers include: simple random sampling; systematic random sampling; stratified random sampling.

13 Possible answers include: reliability as they can be replicated; can be used to establish correlations and test a hypothesis; allows a larger sample so the findings can be generalised; detachment means greater objectivity as there is no contact between the researcher and the respondent.

14 Possible answers include: deception; lack of informed consent; lack of right to withdraw for participants; researcher potentially taking part in immoral or illegal activities; potential harm to participants.

15 Possible answers include: not always easy to identify or control variables; not able to study the past; can only use small samples.

16 Hard official statistics are valid as they measure what they set out to measure, whereas soft official statistics may be socially constructed. For example, soft statistics can be manipulated or be based on the subjective opinion of those compiling them.

17 Possible answers include: they may be in the public domain, making them quick and easy to obtain; cheap; they may be the only way of studying the past.

18 Possible answers include: participant observation; unstructured interviews; group interviews.

19 Verification is proving your own theory right whereas falsification is proving someone else's theory wrong.

20 Possible answers include: formula funding; exam league tables; opting out; open enrolment; business sponsorship of schools.

Index

Note: **bold** page numbers indicate where definitions of key terms can be found.